COME ~~BACK OF~~
& RETURN TO
COMMON
LAW

FROM THE PERSPECTIVE OF AN AWAKENED GOD CONSCIOUS ETERNAL HUMAN BEING

COMMON LAW IS SIMPLY COMMON SENSE
&
LOGIC
BASED ON MORALITY

BY
LOVELIFELEE

PAGE INDEX AT BACK OF BOOK

Published in 2020 by FeedARead.com Publishing

A CIP catalogue record for this title is available from the British Library.

OTHER BOOKS BY LOVELIFELEE

**THE SCAFFOLDING OF LIFE
THE WONDERFUL WORLD OF
GEOMETRIC MATTER
THE BUILDING BLOCKS
OF ALL BIOLOGICAL LIFE &
OUR UNIVERSE
ACCESS THE BLUE PRINT IN
YOUR DNA
GROW A RAINBOW LIGHT BODY
STOP KARMIC CYCLES & EVOLVE
TRANSCEND TIME & SPACE
ASCENSION YOU WILL ACHIEVE
BY LOVE LIFE LEE**

THE SCAFFOLDING OF LIFE
THE BUILDING BLOCKS OF SACRED GEOMETRY
LEARN THE SECRETS OF OUR PHYSICAL UNIVERSE
AND BIOLOGICAL MAKE UP OF OUR DNA, HOW TO
EVOLVE CONSCIOUSLY TRANSCEND TIME & SPACE
TO LEARN HOW TO TRANSVERSE THE
UNIVERSE WITH THOUGHT MIND BODY & SPIRIT
USING YOUR CONSCIOUS ENERGY
USING YOUR LIFE FORCE
UNDERSTAND YOUR FULL POTENTIAL GROW
A NEW BODY INTO BEING CONSCIOUSLY EVOLVE
AND ASCEND CREATE A RAINBOW BODY OF
LIGHT YOUR DIVINE RIGHT

FRONT COVER

3

WISDOM OF MAGICAL WONDER
WISDOM MAGICAL IN NATURE
WISDOM OF SPLENDOUR
FROM THE MINDS EYE & HEART SPACE

OF LOVE LIFE LEE

THROUGH THIS BOOK MESSAGES OF ANCIENT
KNOWLEDGE AND WISDOM ABOUT ACCESSING
YOUR FULLEST POTENTIAL AS A HUMAN BEING
LEARNING TO ACCESS YOUR DNA THROUGH
DISCIPLINE'S PRACTICE'S MEDITATION YOGA
SHAMANIC CEREMONIES PLANT MEDICINES
AYAHUASCA CEREMONIES ASTAL TRAVEL
DREAMS SPIRIT WORLD DIET PART OF THE KEY
AND EVOLVE CONSCIOUSLY GROW A BODY OF LIGHT
FROM THE BLUE PRINT IN YOUR DNA
TRANSCEND TIME AND SPACE
TRANSVERSE THE UNIVERSE TRAVEL THE
HYPER-DIMENSIONAL MATRIX IN YOUR RAINBOW
BODY OF LIGHT
YOU ARE AN IMMORTAL INTERDIMENSIONAL LIGHT
BEING OF ULTRA VIOLET CONSCIOUSNESS ENERGY
ANGELIC DIVINE INFINITE YOU BE
IN AN OCEAN OF LIGHT IN THE ONENESS OF THE
WHOLE CREATION

Spiritual knowledge of the journey
Within and without gaining the understanding
of the scaffolding of life the building blocks of the magical
world of geometric matter the dodecahedrons & tetrahedrons
and life force energy of our selfs and our universe understand
frequencies light vibration in sacred geometry it's wisdom
connecting to the stars
Connecting to nature
Connecting to Energy fields
An awakening , the shaman and i am
A spirit being
An Immortal Interdimensional Light Being
OF Conscious Energy
Divine we be you and me by Divine Decree
Namaste
Blessings to all that be in the oneness of all the creation

BACK COVER

4

THE SCAFFOLDING OF LIFE

THE SCAFFOLDING OF LIFE THE
WONDERFUL WORLD OF
GEOMETRIC MATTER THE
BUILDING BLOCKS OF ALL
BIOLOGICAL LIFE & OUR
UNIVERSE ACCESS THE BLUE
PRINT IN YOUR DNA GROW A
RAINBOW LIGHT BODY STOP
KARMIC CYCLES & EVOLVE
TRANSCEND TIME & SPACE
ASCENSION YOU WILL ACHIEVE

The scaffolding of life the wonderful
world of geometric matter this book
gives information on how to access and
open your eternal immortal light body,
On the building blocks of matter how
your avatar your body is built and that
of the reality around you it explains
how the scaffolding of life is built
through the building blocks of
geometry, and the energies behind it
the driving forces, behind the nucleus,

electrons and black holes, the forces of electromagnetism, gravity, the weak and strong nuclear forces.

It explains how to stop the cycles of life and death to open your eternal light body, via diet, disciplines, and supplements and via monatomic elements the eight colloidal metals we have at birth in our bodies and never get again through food or water.

It explains the sacred geometric matter shapes of how the cells are built by dodecahedrons and their relationship to amino acids and of the tetrahedrons in side the dodecahedrons that relate to the proteins from our intake of food our diet. Also discussed are power planets and their access to the universe, other dimensions of reality in the hyper-dimensional matrix of creation.

The language of the building blocks of life are discussed, our luminous energy fields around are bodies that is the software that informs the hardware the DNA to grow the avatar the body. The torus fields are discussed, also the illusion of light in our universe the university for souls to experience and grow spiritually, the mandelbhrot fractal the building structure of our physical universe is explained via a complex mathematical numbers, also the five geometric shapes are looked at and their relationship to sound, vibrational frequencies.

The chakras the keys to the life force systems and to access travel in the energetic holographical universe are touched on, the energy wave of ascension is looked at, along with DNA upgrade, the law of one, breath control, diet, plant medicines, religious dogma and the shamanic Munay-Ki rites of initiation are discussed, and ascension, our bodies and the universe is a puzzle to be solved, to evolve and transverse.

MEDITATION
THE KEY TO
PEACEFUL
MANIFESTATION
ALLOWING ACCESS
TO YOUR
LIGHTBODY

BY
LOVE LIFE LEE

FRONT COVER

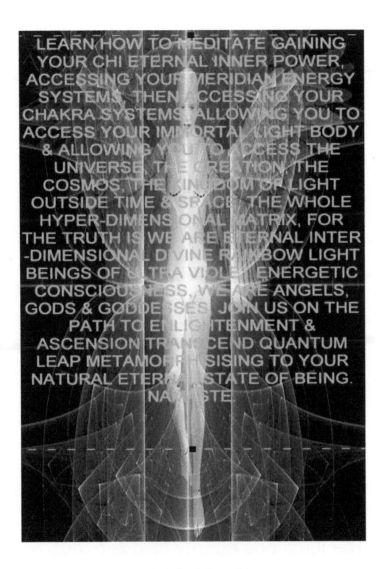

LEARN HOW TO MEDITATE GAINING YOUR CHI ETERNAL INNER POWER, ACCESSING YOUR MERIDIAN ENERGY SYSTEMS, THEN ACCESSING YOUR CHAKRA SYSTEMS, ALLOWING YOU TO ACCESS YOUR IMMORTAL LIGHT BODY & ALLOWING YOU TO ACCESS THE UNIVERSE, THE CREATION, THE COSMOS, THE KINGDOM OF LIGHT OUTSIDE TIME & SPACE, THE WHOLE HYPER-DIMENSIONAL MATRIX, FOR THE TRUTH IS WE ARE ETERNAL INTER -DIMENSIONAL DIVINE RAINBOW LIGHT BEINGS OF ULTRA VIOLET ENERGETIC CONSCIOUSNESS, WE ARE ANGELS, GODS & GODDESSES, JOIN US ON THE PATH TO ENLIGHTENMENT & ASCENSION TRANSCEND QUANTUM LEAP METAMORPHOSISING TO YOUR NATURAL ETERNAL STATE OF BEING. NAMASTE

BACK COVER

MEDITATION THE KEY TO PEACEFUL MANIFESTATIONS

Meditation is the key to peaceful manifestations, then your inner peaceful thoughts will manifest outwards into vibratory words and actions, creating your physical reality of your choosing. Through stillness of the mind with breath work, and ancient breath practices, you will create space to have clarity. With clarity you will see the mind is just a tool of the human avatars, the human biological body in which we manifest, through the luminous energy field around around the human body, which is the software that informs the hardware the DNA to grow the body. The luminous energy field is a foot below your feet, a foot above your head and as wide as your arms stretch outwards.

Learn how to meditate gaining your chi

eternal inner power accessing your meridian energy systems, then accessing your chakra systems allowing you to access your immortal light body and allowing you to access the universe, the creation, the cosmos, the kingdom of light outside time and space, accessing the whole hyper-dimensional matrix, for the truth is, we are eternal inter-dimensional divine rainbow light beings of ultra violet energetic consciousness we are angels, goddesses and gods. Please come join us on the path to enlightenment and ascension, transcend, quantum leap metamorphosing to your natural eternal state of being, namaste LoveLifeLee.

1

UNDERSTANDING HOW & WHY STATUTE LAW & COMMON LAW WERE CREATED

THE DECEIT OF WORDS USED IN LAW

The illegitimate unlawful imperative criminal laws, civil laws, citations that are rules of action imposed upon mere by some authority which enforces obedience to it and there are two kinds of imperative laws, Divine or Human law, (but are they really universal and human law considering the fact that humanity was invaded by the extraterrestrial fallen angel bloodlines thousands of years ago and they have pushed these false illegitimate unlawful laws into humanities society). The illegitimate unlawful laws being against established and accepted rules and standards of Constitutional Law which is Natural Law and also Universal Law, these unlawful laws that come from the criminal state the corporate government and all their agencies from their criminal institutions, these laws are unlawful and criminal from the royal descendants of the fallen angel bloodlines, of blood sacrifice they are a blood cult, that worship Ca'an the God of blood sacrifice and the God Molock the God of child sacrifice, Molock is the biblical name of a Canaanite God associated with child sacrifice through fire and war, they make laws up for humanities citizens while they do the opposite commiting the sickest of crimes against humanities children of pedophilia, the rape and torture of children for the adrenaline fuelled blood they consume called Adrenochrome, the sin of all sins whether you are perceiving it from a mortal or immortal perspective of consciousness.

These criminal unlawful laws enforced and administered by the government agencies of the blood cults corporate private army called the police forces and other enforcing agencies of the royal blood cult, for in the past it was Peace Officers that were good men and women that served the local communites and worked with their local native citizens, but now you have a royal blood cult of corporate police enforcers.

Common Law is nothing to do with any government, the real true Law of the Land, it is a simple system of law meaning to not harm by not causing physical injury or mental damage or hurt, to do no evil, to do no wrong, to do no morally wrong injury, there are in fact two different systems of law that are Statute Law and Common Law, so you need to learn and understand Common Law as this will allow you to separate from the illegally enforced and imposed Statute unlawful Laws and to disconnect for your personal selfs, family, friends and your businesses.

So where did Statute Law come from, it came from Law of the Sea, who set it up and what are Statute Laws what do they actually mean, the old law, Law of the Sea that now makes Statute Law was created and evolved when commerce between nations between countries came into being, this is when the sailing merchant ships were trading in commerce and under Law of the Sea, so the fallen angel bloodlines created laws for this trading and commerce of all varieties of goods, that were Corporate Laws and these Corporate Laws were only relevant or appropriated within this trading of goods commerce system, that the fallen bloodlines set up and orchestrated into being into reality.

Now these sailing vessels and larger merchant ships all flew flags and many nations had different laws, the flags let others know the law in which the sailing vessels and their occupants were obeying and operating under, if a flag had a gold trim around the edge of the flag you are operating under the Law of Contracts, the Corporate Law, Law of the Sea, which is

Admiralty Law, if you boarded, and entered a certain vessel then these laws you would be obliged to follow, it was know as Admiralty or Maritime Law also commonly known as Law of the Sea, this is the body of law that governs nautical issues and private maritime disputes.

So Admiralty Law consists of both domestic law on maritime activities and private international law governing the relationships between private parties operating or using ocean going ships. So then if we go back we can see that the royal fallen angels and their descendants of the blood sacrifice cult then decided with their knavish ways to over ride and dismiss the Common Law of the People, the earth citizens, the Common Law of the natural living man, the law of embodied eternal divine light being immortal souls incarnated in a human biological avatar, from outside time and space in the eternal realms of the Kingdom of Light.

These fallen royal bloodlines of the blood sacrifice cult then started to replace and remove the Maritime Law of the sea and create and bring in Statute Law, which the truth be known as the Laws of Contracts, these Statute Laws you need to know and understand are where you have to have two corporate entities, that is a thing a person a group a company a corporation with distinct and independent existence, so an establishment, a body, organization, institution, a structure that is in existence, living, being, life, animation of therefore of or in our physical reality, these contracts between at least two entities have to be contractual in a way that is agreed upon in or enforce by a contract, you have to agree on certain factures and structure in place, you have to have an agreement in place between both or more of the parties of entities involved.

So we then can perceive that the fallen angel royal blood cult has deceived all of humanity for so long by illusions of contracts, the illusion of words through the Laws of the Sea now changed into Statute Corporate Law the Law of Contracts, and through there knavish ways and through their language of SPELLS the language of words of twisted politics, they weave their dark magic by these dark negative witches and dark magician from the royal blood cult. The thing is though is that you can only have jurisdiction the official power to make legal decisions and judgements over one or the other of parties of entities or entity if you are in a contract, if both the two have agreed upon within two entities or more an agreement and therefore created a contract, this is the law of the fallen angels bloodlines cult and the law of their puppet goverments, corporations, entities, companies, deceiving charities, churches and more.

So the enforcers the corrupt politians, judges the police force they get frustrated and even aggressive and angry when you don't play their game of the language of words the language of spells, and you stand up in the Tongue of Common Law and understand Statute Law, you can then not fall for their mind tricks of knavish intentioned words of laws, their trickery that they use and try to deceive you, into being in contract, to being in agreement via the interaction and with the SPELLS of words, to try to BIND you into a contract, they say and repeat as part of the polices mantra do you understand me, over and over, this they try to trick you into Statute Law, Corporate Law, its then you must say to the police in that present moment, ARE YOU UNDER OATH OFFICER YES OR NO, then say NO I do not understand you , I do (not-stand) under you, I am a Sentient Spiritual Being of Light I am in the present manifested in this human biological avatar body, for this life times experience, I am a natural living breathing man/woman living under the Eternal Common Law, also bound by Universal Law, Karmic Law and bound

19

by Law of Attraction. So therefore gentlemen you are not dealing with a fictitious corporate entity I do not consent contract with you, for I have accessed God Consciousness, therefore good day may you be blessed eternally, namaste. You need to know and understand that in the English language, Do You Understand, means do you comprehend what I am saying to you?. But in the trickery language of Legalese it has been changed to actually mean, Do you stand under me?, actually meaning, DO YOU GRANT ME AUTHORITY OVER YOU SO THAT YOU HAVE TO OBEY WHATEVER I TELL YOU TO DO!

So this means if you do not consent, do not contract with them they have no jurisdiction over you, for you are claiming your own Sovereignty and that you are not a corporate entity, and their language of words, of spells to deceive you into being in contract, trying to trick you into being an owned fictitous entity in enslavement, by an extraterrestrial fallen angel royal Goldsmith Davidic Israelite bloodlines, a blood cult of of child sacrifice, of dark black negative magicians and witches, as they be casting their negative spells over humanity. So then we start to perceive the true reality of Statute Law and how and where it came from, that they took the law of Admiralty or Maritime Law most commonly known as Law of the Sea, the Corporate Law the Law of Contracts, the deceit and trickery of spell words used to spell bind you into contract into their covernant, of blood sacrifice, for dark art magicians and witches they be weaving their spells of negative intentioned chi energy, to suppress and control the eternal immortal interdimensional light being angel souls that are incarnated in a biological human body avatar, on this planet Gaia our Mother Earth Pachamama, so wake up to who you truly are the eternal God conscious divine being and connect to nature, to spirit, to energy, connect to your soul within via your unconscious mind and your conscious mind via meditation, diet, spiritual practices, ceremonies, energy arts, yoga, martial arts, qi-gong, healing practices, then you can manifest and you can weave your own controlled positive vibrations of light spells of wonder of pure magic in nature, via the sacred building blocks of life through our words and spells within them, the language of words the language of spells that creates all manifested matter into creation.

So they just moved these laws on to the lands, so Maritime Law, Law of the Sea is what is governing citizens of the world today, by force by their unwelcome decision or ruling on someone, on a citizen who is an eternal sentient being of light, manifested in a biological human avatar, living as a natural living breathing man/woman for Angels and Goddesses and Gods we truly be, then you awaken and see and perceive from your accessed God consciousness, that this is the true illusion that this cult of royal dark witches and dark magicians in league with negative races the Draco and with negative energy beings from the $4^{th}/5^{th}$ densities, the Archons the Jinn, the devils and demons they be for a satanic blood cult of sacrifice they are, trying to stop humanity and the eternal souls within from manifesting sacred geometric matter the building blocks of the scaffolding of life, in all forms of sentient life and our surrounding realities.

They try to SPELL BIND humanity into slavery, to spell bind you with the language of letters meaning magical powerful manifesting symbols, within the language of words the language of spells, to not connect with all in the ONENESS in the creation in the hyper-dimensional matrix of realities, of the cosmos inside time and space in these holographical light universities and to stop you accessing outside time and space in the eternal realms the kingdom of light we call home, this is a multidimensional spiritual war for your souls enslavement or for your feedom by accessing your light body via the schematics of a blue print within your DNA, you access this consciously and do ceremonies, diet spiritual practices, then you can ascend being fully embodied on 4th/5th dimensional earth and able to travel in the stars with your MER-KA-BA human light body, opening a sixty foot ball of light around your being and travel through the portholes of the suns from solar system to solar system or galaxy to galaxy or you can just teleport at will instantaneously any where in Creation, the Brahman, the Whole, for negative SPELLS cannot bound you any longer for God conscious you shall be.

Under Statute Law, Law of the Sea it only applies between contracting corporations, that is why the legal language used are terms related to the Law of the Sea, so when the fallen angel bloodlines moved the Law of the Sea on land they made all governements and these underlying agencies of the councils, child welfare, social sevices, the fire sevice, the police, privately owned corporations, therefore using trickery and negative magical SPELLS to entrap you into a contract, and our parents were victims to this and unknowingly enrolled us in the blood cults slavery system when they got birth certificates for us as infants, and the corporations made up a fictitious entity and labelled and attached that to us via the birth certificate for your life time, our parents were tricked and deceived by the deceit of the blood cult, so therefore this is Invalid and Legally Null & Void and has no value therefore no legal force, no substance of energy behind it, because the fictitious entities also known as your Strawman can only be created by putting MRS, MISS, MASTER, MR in front of your name, so your illegal unlawful corporate entity name would be MR LOVELIFELEE, but my sentient conscious natural breathing living man name would just be lovelifelee.

So therefore the attachment is via the understanding that if you acknowledge you are a person then you are owned by a corporate entity of the royal blood cult, and at the same time their dark witches and dark magicians cast their evil dark spells to create an illusion and trick you the eternal God conscious soul residing in this biological human avatar, living as a living breathing natural man/woman, into believing you are this entity of a corporation by calling you Miss, Mrs, Master, Mr in front of your natural living breathing man name, in Capital Letters, magicians trickery via the language of words the language of spells of letters with magical symbolic spiritual manifesting powers.

You are programmed, indoctrinated and brain washed from birth, manipulated on multidimensional levels, the illegitimate unlawful illegal cult corporate entities need to get you to contract via these false fictitious entity character attachments that they prescribe, and made up out of thin air and are attached, to the governments and their agencies, these fictitious entity attachments prescribed to you, a sentient eternal God conscious living breathing man/women sentient being of light. This then allows them to impose their will against the living breathing man/woman that is deceived and admits they are a fictitious person, by saying or agreeing they are a Miss, Mrs, Master, Mr therefore entering into a contract with the corporate entities owned by the fallen royal angel bloodlines blood sacrifice cult, and you do this unconsciously because of the many layers on multidimensional levels of their deceit, deception, trickery, evil intent of manifesting negative dark magic energetic spells of manifesting creative divine chi energy, to create the greatest illusion, an illusion of illusions, to blind you and bind you by the language of law via the language of words the language of spells. They have created an illusion that they the cult and their governments agencies enforcers have power over you, they have NONE you are a Sentient God/Goddess conscious living breathing man/woman, living under Universal Common Law they have no jurisdiction over your Sovereignty as a sentient eternal being manifested into a human avatar body, for you the soul are not the body or mind, these are tools to operate our biological systems and used to manifest our surrounding realities, this is the elite cults game by using spells the covenant uses illusions on top of illusions of trickery from dark magic spells they cast into humanities consciousness and into the creation, the biggest ever False Flag operation conducted on humanity, on earths population, the magnitude of their crimes is beyond belief of the illegitimate unlawful Statute Law of corrupt corporate laws to the programmed indoctrinated and brainwashed citizens of humanity, that have been tricked to think that the false fabricated corporate entity person of MR LOVELIFELEE, that they illegitimately unlawfully illegally created is the sentient living breathing man/woman, but they are not the same and to those slowly waking up consciously, we start to realise and understand these laws do not apply to us Sentient living light beings, they have no weight or power of jurisdiction over the Sovereignty of your being, the audacity and the insanity of the royal fallen extraterrestrial angels and their descendants blood sacrifice cults trickery and crimes is madness, and so 26000 to 78000 years of karmatic debt they will pay of suffering on a continuum of life time after life time until their karmic debt is payed in full, NAMASTE AMEN.

It is all an farce a huge illusion of spells cast for control by an invading extraterrestrial fallen angel royal bloodlines of a dying blood cult, that's losing grip and control on all levels and in all structures of our societies, for the illusion is over, as the Ascension energy wave returns to our solar system and consciousness will be raised for the souls that are ready to ascend, and the lower vibrational souls will be harvested and be placed in another 3rd dimensional 26000 year expeience, for spiritual growth and karmatic debts to be payed in full.

So what is this structure of this entity of the justice system, it is not separate and independant from the privately owned fallen angel royal bloodline cult of dark negative witches and dark magicians that cast and use dark spell binding corporations they own, the governments and its justice system, the courts and judges are working for corporate interest not on behalf of the world Eternal Sentient Human living breath man/woman citizens, so most of the world wide citizens don't even know the positions they hold in these government institutions, and entities are doing the negative deeds and casings of negative spells over humanity, they the states employees like police, judges and all the other deparments and services other corporations, don't even know they are working for a blood sacrifice cult, a coven of extraterrestrial negative witches and dark wizards, dark magicians, working against humanities co-creative consciousness and that of every Sentient soul individually on earth, by casting dark spells of negative intent by using the building blocks of life, sacred geometric matter, to trick humanity into manifesting through our individual and co-creative conscious thoughts an illusion of reality, and so now we see their knavish spells and through their deceit and their trickery.

So how have they cast spells on you and tricked you and deceived you because you are born on this planet Gaia, our Mother Earth, Pachamama, a Sentient immortal light being of conscious ultra violet energetic God consciousness, born into a human biological avatar, therefore you are born a living breathing human child to become a living breathing woman/man, this means that a biological living child, woman, man cannot be owned by any corporate entity, so Statute Law is Nullified has no meaning or power over a Sentient Eternal God conscious living breathing human being ·

an individual entity, because we are not a corporate entity, we are divine angels we are Immortal Goddesses and Gods, we are God conscious Eternal light beings of the Oneness energetic co-creative divine cosmic consciousness, casting our spells of peace love light and magic and weaving positive light energy into the fabric of time and space, if humanity was not hindered and held in a low vibration by a false illusion of reality created by the bloodlines of blood sacrifice, these royal fallen Goldsmith Davidic Israelite invading extraterrestrial blood sacrifice cult, are an infestation on earth and the less than one percent that they represent on the planet in the population of earth, is so minute we can use positive magic on them, so become a magician, a witch of energy and cast your spells to dispel them from the planet Gaia our Mother Earth, Pachamana and dispel them out of existence in the whole creation the brahman the whole.

You need to understand that at the top of

the Masonic judisial system and top of
the Masonic police forces the corrupt cult
members, they know they are using the
illegitimate unlawful illusion of corrupt
Statute Law, Law of the Sea and that it
does not apply to the world citizens
unless they trick you by casting spells in
the language of words, to spell bind you
into a contract with the corporate cult
coven of blood sacrifice, then enslaving
you and your children unlawfully, so
illegally and criminally imprisoning you
by force even for the pettiest of supposed
illegal offences that do not apply to you
the Sentient living breathing man/woman.

These lower normal police officers and
other officers of these of the Statute Law
blood sacrifice cult, some have no idea
they are administering Corporate Law,
they does not apply to world sentient
human citizens of earth, they may have
no idea these police enforcing officers
that they actually work for a royal
extraterrestrial fallen angels blood
sacrifice coven, working for a half breed

child sacrificing pedophilia cult, of child rapists and murders feeding of the loosh energy of humanities co-creative conscious energy, and feeding off of humanities children literally, by way of their addiction to Adrenochrome, which is childrens blood full of adrenaline, after the child is tortured, these extraterrestrial Draco and half breed bloodlines, trick humanities police enforcing officers and other officers of the blood cult enforcers into commiting crimes on the worlds cosmic Sentient Eternal living breathing men/woman divine entity citizens, they are crimes the police officers are commiting as they have no power, no jurisdiction over a divine immortal interdimensional light being of Sentient Eternal ultra violet God conscious energy, for we have Sovereignty over our own divine energetic consciousness and that of our manifested biological human avatar bodies. The officers don't understand Statute Laws true intent of magic spells that it casts, and that they are regulating direct control and conducting and managing and handling the illegitimate unlawful Statute law, so Corporate Law for the will of the extraterrestrial blood sacrifice coven of the fallen angel goldsmith Davidic Israelite demonic satanic blood cult, the judges and officers and police officers have been deceived to work against their own human race, to go against their own species, via trickery of the language of words the language of SPELLS, and that they the officers are going against Common Law, Law of the Land, Natural Law, Universal Law, Karmatic Law and Law of Attraction, when they subvert the will of sentient eternal earth living breathing man/woman earth citizens, with the crimes the officers commit of assault battery and even murder on a regular basis, they all the officers and police officers of the corporate blood cult will pay with Law of Attraction, every person they have man handled or assaulted or worse will come back to them in this life or in the next life times or ones to follow, and they will experience what they

35

physically, mentally and emotional did to others, this is the way of Universal Law, the Karmic Law of cause and effect of spells cast by the language of words the language of spells and by your actions and interactions, these unconscious programmed, indoctrinated and brain washed officers, commit illegal acts when trying to impose their will on the earth citizens and as they commit crimes daily on Sentient living breathing divine eternal human light beings on earth, many or some of them unwittingly on the general public eternal citizens on earth. Some have no idea as they lay out charges and citations they give you a preprogrammed narrative of illegitimate unlawful Corporate Law that's Statute Law, Law of the Sea, not applicable to a Sovereign God Conscious Eternal Light Being residing in an avatar of biological human construct created by your divine energetic chi God conscious energy.

So I say right now in the present and daily be still meditate find silence and

then clarity will come, stillness will ensue
then you can visulize and connect your
crown chakra to source energy allowing
cosmic white light energy to pour into
your entire being filling your luminous
energy field, then you can connect your
base chakra to your mother earths chakra
receiving your mothers nourishment of
energy filling your luminous energy field,
then you are able to connect a filament of
white light from your third eye chakra to
your heart chakra this will then allow you
to now produce, ultra violet light
conscious energy from your heart chakra,
you can then direct your ultra violet
divine energetic chi consciousness,
energy in any direction, in any place in
space and time and outside time
and space in the eternal realms of the
Kingdom of Light, this is the most
powerful vibration and density of cosmic
eternal divine energetic chi light of the
oneness, of the co-created God conscious
eternal sea of light energy.
So I say weave your positive spells of
eternal chi light energy into the fabric of

time and space daily, to counter act this royal fallen angel blood sacrificing cults spells, that they cast by their dark negative witches and dark magicians that are in contract with coven of demons and devils, the Archons the Jinn. Then weaving your own spells of light you can dispell their negative casted spells and go beyond and counter them and join forces with other, light workers and unite your chi energy co-creative consciousness and direct it towards the cult and its bloodlines, visualize that they do not even exist in our reality and dispel them and cast them from existence, we can achieve this by starting to become united with groups of eight or more, for a power energetic force eight connected in co-creative chi conscious energy, understand it takes only three God conscious human eternal light beings manifested on earth to join their three co-creating consciousness and they can create an entire solar system with their thought energy chi united as One, it may even be possible for three beings to create an entire star cluster like ours consisting of fifty two solar systems, all is possible for I truly believe that each one of us can create an entire universe into being with our own single cell individual eternal God consciousness via accessing the oneness of all consciousness, in the cosmos the creation the brahman the whole.

For we are angels of manifesting chi light energy, divine we be on a continuum of evolution metamorphosising, ascending, transcending, quantum leaping of creating all of the oneness that be, that we are intrinsically in a natural and in an essential way, connected to in all dimensions and densities of light that are woven into the fabric of time and space, and woven into the eternal immortal realms outside time and space, our true home in the kingdom of light, so weave your magical chi light energy, cast spells of positive intention for all sentient life and cast spells to protect your kin your families and cast spells to diminish and distinguish the energy and entities of the royal fallen bloodlines, and their allies the

Draco reptilians, the Archons the Jinn the $4^{th}/5^{th}$ density energetic beings of demons and devils, cast light weave it into the fabric of time and space via spells and bring into being their demise from existence, for humanity will then be free from tyranny, or just focus on a collective vison of the future of humanity with plentiful for all with magic beauty and wonder all living in harmony as one collective and then humanity can manifest their light bodies and travel in the stars at will, living once again life as a fully embodied human being, but eternally free connected to the oneness that be truly, accessing the stars and travelling in the hyper-dimensional matrix of creation in the cosmoses entirety, Namaste Amen.

2

COMMON LAW RESPONSES WHEN INTERACTING WITH ILLEGITIMATE UNLAWFUL CORPORATE STATUTE LAW OFFICERS

These rights are given to you at birth under NATURAL LAW.
So if you understand and know the law of the CONSTITUTIONAL LAW which is the bases of the English legal system and across the world.

Under NATURAL LAW you have these rights that can never be taken away from you, you also have a hierarchy of laws which are and is NATURAL LAW –

THE RULE OF LAW – Then the people.

THEN THE PEOPLE – Bring government into existence – Then various arms of government – Parliament then Judiciary the system of courts that adjudicates legal disputes and interprets, defends and applies law in legal cases.

In CONSTITUTIONAL LAW – The Government is brought into existence by THE PEOPLE – But it is known that the main three tiers of government cannot bring in or create any ACTS, STATUES, GUIDELINES, or any REGULATIONS – That can INFRINGE on NATURAL LAW rights, so cannot be encroached upon in a way that violates NATURAL LAW – This means corporate statue officers enforcing criminal and illegitimate unlawful corporate Statute Law cannot Impringe their will on you as to impinge is to come into contact or encroach or have an impact and to infringe is to encroach on a right or privilege or to violate THE NATURAL LAW RIGHTS we receive from BIRTH. Infringe as a verb abuse of a privilege, abuse of one's rights, advance stealthily (meaning deception of words to get you into and illegitimate unlawful corporate Statute Law contract by trickery of words deceit there game), aggress, arrogate, breach, break bounds, break upon, break into, commit a CRIME against our BIRTH given NATURAL LAW rights, our INALIENABLE RIGHTS.

So NATURAL LAW rights which are INALIENABLE rights, which are (PERSONAL RIGHTS that cannot be ignored), given to us citizens of humanity on this planet Gaia our Mother Earth, Pachamama, these rights are given to us at birth and can never be taken away and those freedoms and rights include – FREE SPEECH – FREEDOM TO THINK – FREEDOM OF ASSOCIATION – FREEDOM OF ASSEMBLY – BODY INTEGRITY and access to JUSTICE – These rights CAN NEVER BE TAKEN AWAY.

So you the individual start using these rights and INVOKE them when interacting with criminal illegitimate corporate Statute Law enforcing officers, by always starting with – ARE YOU

UNDER OATH OFFICER, ARE YOU
ACTING UNDER YOUR OATH of
CONSTITUTIONAL LAW, YOUR
OATH OF COMMON LAW, YOU'RE
YOUR OATH OF NATURAL LAW –
Which is UNIVERSAL LAW, yes or no
officer.

Every citizen in government which is
four tiers down, they have to SWEAR an
OATH to up hold the constitutions, and
the constitutions are brought into
Existence under NATURAL LAW –
which is stated in the history of LAW –
That all government can bring in nothing
that can INFRINGE on our FREEDOMS
– To Speech, to Think, of association or
assembly, to travel, of justice and body
integrity.

3

WHAT TO SAY TO THE ILLEGITIMATE UNLAWFUL CRIMINAL CORPORATION ENFORCER POLICE OFFICER & OTHER ENFORCING AGENTS

When interacting with the criminal corporation enforcing officers – You would say to them – ARE YOU ACTING UNDER OATH OFFICER – If they do not answer which many do not and try to avoid answering, YOU SAY – YES or NO are you acting under OATH officer, then some times there Ego gets bruised and then if an officer trys to arrest you and detain you, YOU SHOULD SAY – I'M GOING TO VIDEO YOU – They will say you can not video me, they will even say in certain locations, you can't film me in this train station or airport or outside a police station, and then YOU SAY – YES I CAN VIDEO YOU because if you are COMMITING A

CRIME as a SERVANT or CIVIL SERVANT or an OATH TAKER, that get there salary from the government, that we The People the citizens are paying, THEN I CAN FILM, VIDEO and RECORD for preservation for legal DOCUMENT MANUSCRIPT EVIDENCE RECORDS.

Then if the officer insists you cant video film them that they have all these guidelines, YOU SAY – NO NO NO GUIDELINES can not INFRINGE PERSONAL RIGHTS, UNDER CONSTITUTIONAL LAW which you swore an OATH to, which is NATURAL LAW and so by Universal Law.

IF A CRIMINAL CORPORATION ENFORCING OFFICER TRYS TO ARREST & HANDCUFF YOU – THIS IS WHAT TO SAY

When an officer starts to enter your personal space SAY TO THEM – I DO NOT CONSENT, if you touch me with hand cuffs as I've informed you I DO NOT CONSENT, I DO NOT CONSENT TO BEING STOPPED – Then usually an officer will go in front of you or try and block you from movement of physical travel, then YOU SAY – I DO NOT CONSENT TO YOU STOPPING ME and I DO NOT CONSENT TO YOU PHYSICALLY TOUCHING ME, MY BODY, MY PERSON – then YOU SHOULD SAY – If You Put CUFFS On Me That is a CRIME of BATTERY, because I have Rights If YOU PHYSICALLY TOUCH ME or STOP my MOVEMENT, STOP me TRAVELLING, you OFFICER are ACTING OUTSIDE your OATH, that is UNLAWFUL as you know as you took the CONSTITUTIONAL LAW OATH, the OATH of NATURAL LAW, which is UNIVERSAL LAW.

Continue SAYING – ACTING outside of your OATH this is UNLAWFUL – If you touch me or put hand cuffs on me that is a

CRIME of BATTERY which is Five years in prison.

If a Police Officer does something UNLAWFUL – They are actually going outside of their PROTECTION of the POLICE.

If an Officer does not answer that they are under OATH when asked or try to avoid the answer to that question, it then logical to assume that the officer knows that what they are doing is UNLAWFUL, and if an officer admits to doing UNLAWFUL behaviour and therefore COMMITING a CRIME, then they can go to prison for up to TWENTY years, for being in Police Uniform COMMITING a CRIME.

When an officer does not answer that they are under OATH and when they are about to put hand cuffs on, you Film, Video Record them, then SAY – OFFICER YOU ARE NOW ENTERING INTO CONTRACT and MY said hourly RATE IS 5000.00 Pounds an Hour (you can choose any amount as they are

ENTERING into CONTRACT and YOU
DO NOT CONSENT).
Then YOU SAY to the Officer – It will
cost you 5000.00 Pounds an Hour and
there are (if this is the case more than
one officer present) four officers present,
so this RATE will apply personally
individually to each officer present, so the
hourly cost will be 20,000.00 Per Hour, if
you illegally and criminally detain me
without my CONSENT.

If the officer (s) do Commit the Crime of
BATTERY and by doing so also commit
the crime of KIDNAP by illegally and
criminally hand cuffing you without your
Consent and detain you after say three
hours of illegal and criminal detainment,
YOU SHOULD SAY to the officer (s) –
That all officers will be CHARGED the
said RATE of the Initial contact, when I
did not CONSENT and told them that
they were ENTERING CONTRACT with
YOU against your then STATED NON-
CONSENT, and that they are now going
to be charged individually up to this said

time (for three hours of illegitimate unlawful detainment) 15,000.00 Pounds each, so collectively four officers equals 60,000.00 Pound Invoice in total.
As you were told The Said Hourly Rate Cost when you ENTERED into CONTRACT against my CONSENT at the initial contact three hours prior to my illegitimate unlawful and criminal detention, when you ILLEGALLY broke your OATH, so COMMITING a CRIME, One of the Crimes being of Battery, another being the Crime of Kiddnapping.

So next YOU MUST SAY – I ALSO INFORM YOU THAT I WILL NOT BE PAYING ANY FINES as they are UNLAWFUL, and CRIMINAL in nature under NATURAL LAW, (then state the time frame of prison sentence for that Crime and maximum Fine) – I believe its six months in prison and up to a 10,000.00 Fine for that Crime.
Then YOU SHOULD SAY – I WILL BE CHARGING every hour to each individual officer, including preparing the

case, with the Said 5000.00 Pounds Hourly Rate.

Next you need to tell the officers the next procedure after that will be that the case will go to High Court and the Supreme Court and that you will WIN the case, because each officer Acted Unlawful there by Commiting the Crimes of – UNLAWFUL DETENTION, KIDNAPPING, the Crime of BATTERY.

Then YOU SHOULD SAY – And any police officer Acting Under OATH knows that being Additionally dressed up as a police officer, and Acting as an Officer but is Criminally Illegitimately Unlawfully Arresting Citizens is a CRIME so Punishable by up to TWENTY years in Prison.

Be aware that many corporation criminal Statute Law enforcing officers are programmed and heavily indoctrinated and many completely brain washed and ignorant with an illusion of what the real true reality of law is in relation to

Corporation Law, so Statute Law, Law of Contracts coming from Maritime Law so Admiralty Law known commonly as Law of the Sea. To the Relation of LAW of the LAND known as COMMON LAW which is NATURAL LAW which is UNIVERSAL LAW, used by and for Divine Sentient Eternal Light Beings manifesting into Embodied (Human) Avatars and all Species in the Universe.

But sadly also other officers are very conscious of the CONSTITUTIONAL LAW OATH that they took and circumnavigate and weave around it and twist and miss inform citizens of the truth and many just straight out lie and deceive by way of intended Deception, which is a Crime.

Then at the top of command the Masonic Police Officers absolutely know that they are morally wrongly and illegally enforcing illegitimate unlawful criminal Corporate Statute Law, Law of Contracts Birthed from the illigitmate unlawful

Admiralty Law, Law of the Sea, and these Masonic top Officers they are well aware that they are operating illegitimately unlawfully so illegally and Criminally against there OATH of the Constitution, of the LAW OF THE LAND, against NATURAL LAW which is UNIVERSAL LAW.

4

WHAT TO SAY TO ILLEGITIMATE UNLAWFUL CRIMINAL CORPORATE STATUTE ENFORCING OFFICERS WHEN TRAVELLING AT THESE INSANE UNLOGICAL TIMES THROUGH PORTS & AIRPORTS & ON PUBLIC TRANSPORT

So if you are travelling to another country another nation you will have to go through an immigration system, visa system, but you are a person so a citizen of your own country, you have rights to come and rights to travel – This means for no reason can they stop you travelling for personal or for business and especially if you are returning home to your own country your own nation.

So at worldwide ports and airports they have new Illegitimate Unlawful Criminal system where they Tell You to fill out a form, a form called a PASSENGER

LOCATOR FORM, DO NOT FILL
THIS FORM OUT, as if you were to fill
out the passenger locator form – YOU
ARE actually waving your RIGHTS and
AGREEING to LOCK YOUR SELF up,
LIKE a PRISONER in your OWN
HOME for fourteen days, by SIGNING
IT.
This also applies the same if you
DOWNLOAD any APP(s). Online to do
with TRACK OR TRACE, as you are
AUTOMATICALLY ENTERING into
CONTRACT and AGREEING to the
TERMS and said CONDITIONS.

So you do not when travelling have to
wear a face mask or fill out the passenger
locator form this is just a legal fact, so
DO NOT fill the form going onto a fight
and DO NOT download any APP(s).
On your return flight again do not fill out
any passenger locator forms as you DO
NOT CONSENT to CONTRACT via
DECEIT of these Illegitimate Unlawful
Corporate Statute Law that are Criminal
in nature.

On the return flight by not filling the form out just be prepared calmy and ready that they may detain you and you be ready to informed the officers of the procedures that have been layed out in this and previous chapters of this informative book. If they do hold you so illegitimately unlawfully illegally detain and kidnap you, its usually to make a point and pressure you to do something against your true wishes, so against your will, against your INALIENABLE RIGHTS, your BIRTH RIGHTS of CONSTITUTIONAL LAW so NATURAL LAW which is UNIVERSAL LAW via coersion and trickery of words, trickery of language, playing on your fears with intimidation.

So STAND in your POWER as an Eternal Divine Light Being of Ultra Violet Energetic Consciousness that are presently in the moment of Now Embodied in your Biological Human Avatar Body, and SAY NO – Tell the Police Officer(s) NO I AM NOT

FILLING IN THE FORM because I AM INVOKING my INALIENABLE RIGHTS, I AM INVOKING my PERSONAL RIGHTS – Which are NOT BESTOWED by LAW, CUSTOM or BELIEF, which can NOT be TAKEN AWAY or IGNORED by STATUE ENFORCING POLICE OFFICERS.

5

WHAT TO SAY TO CRIMINAL CORPORATE STATUTE LAW ENFORCER OFFICERS CONCERNING UNLAWFUL FACE MASKS

So you NEVER have to WEAR a FACE MASK they are UNCONSTITUTIONAL UNLAWFUL and quite frankly ridiculous, for with common sense and simple logic a supposed virus (as I don't believe viruses exist as there has never ever been a virus isolated in any experiment on the planet, they lied to world citizens, but biological chemical injection weapons do exist and given FAKE virus names but are in fact biological weapons made in laboratories, by for example mixing two animal tissues which are mutated cells, like a cow with leukemia and sheep with mutated cancer cells mixing them with chemicals and injected into a person and told they will prevent an illusionary virus, as it's actually a biological weapon and the next stronger strain of the supposed virus, so a bio-weapon is in the supposed Non-Vaccine Biological Chemical Injection for prevention supposedly, but its not its to spread the next stronger mutated strain of the biological weapon they created in citizens in world society, this is in several of my other books) can be spread airbourne via biological air spores so cell fragments, but masks don't work it preposterous really its madness.

One main thing many of the world citizens do not know is when wearing a mask your not taking in enough or the right amount of oxygen into the brain this is causing neurological damage to the brain therefore slowing brain clarity, brain function and bodily function, in action and reaction functions, also keeping in bad bacteria normally expelled from the body via clear breathing pathways the mouth and nasal cavity, this bad bacteria stays in the lungs causing dis-ease, so creates lung infections. Now regarding illegitimate unlawful corporate Statute Law enforcing officers and wearing face masks, and what your response should be when approached and encroached on by illegitimate unlawful corporate Statute Law officers, DO NOT give CONSENT to there requests, as said before always ask if the officer or officers are UNDER OATH and SAY – Officer are you UNDER OATH and are you ACTING UNDER OATH YES or NO officer – then if you have a MEDICAL condition tell them – I have a MEDICAL condition I an EXEMPT from wearing a face mask. The police cannot ask you what your medical condition is as they break a couple of Laws. You need to verbal SAY – I INVOKE my INALIENABLE RIGHTS from birth that you officers cannot IGNORE, and can never be taken away or recroached upon by LAW, CONSTITUTIONAL LAW which is NATURAL LAW which is UNIVERSAL LAW, so no one can coheres you or threaten you even the Corporate Statute Law enforcement officers, that are acting outside of their powers and acting outside of their sworn OATH of CONSTITUTIONAL LAW which is COMMON LAW, which means you are committing a crime and wearing a police officers uniform which is up to twenty years in prison and a maximum fine of ten thousand pounds.

Say I DO NOT GIVE CONSENT and walk away if they try to stop you, follow the procedure in the previous chapters of this book, Film them commiting Crime and if they go to arrest you inform them of NO CONSENT to touch you physically, and if they cuff you it's the crime of BATTERY and they will be entering into CONTRACT and say your hourly rate of five thousand pounds or higher amount if you so wish.

It is well known, and just common sense and logic that we need oxygen to live and masks variably and clearly reduce oxygen levels to absolute dangerous levels, and therefore it increases your carbon dioxide levels. When we breath in normally in our standard breathing rythum, inhale the in breath and exhale the out breath its about four hundred parts per million which is in the air we breathe, but after wearing a face mask for a few minutes the carbon dioxide levels that you are exhaling are at and higher toxic levels, that are around two thousand parts per million, and can rise up to six thousand parts per million, tests have shown up to thirteen thousand parts per million wearing a mask, this is Highly Dangerous, Not Safe and will cause Neurological issues and after only two hours wearing a face mask from studies you can get irreverseable damage to the brain.

In health regulations if you are working in an environment with two thousand parts per million it is considered unsafe. This means the toxic levels of carbon dioxide are poisoning there bodies and minds, so wearing a mask means you are literally poisoning your self, toxifing your mind and body, causing Dis-ease, so Disease which will form in the body especially the lungs, with the reduction of Oxygen you can get nausea, headaches, migrans, and chronic fatigue.

Another thing to know about face masks is 2,300 years ago, long before Islam, Arabs discovered that forcing people to cover their noses and mouths broke their will and individuality, and depersonalized them, it made them submissive.
That is why they later imposed on every WOMAN the mandatory use of a fabric over her face, then Islam turned it into the woman's symbol of submission to Allah, the man owner of the Harem, and the King.
Modern psychology explains without a face we don't exist as independent beings.
Face coverings, face masks are ancient tools used to break people down psychologically, this is the beginning of deleting individuality, he who does not

know his or her history is certainly condemned to repeat it.
I see through the veil past the illusion of deception, I percieve and read the energy frequency of Lucifer in the Luminous Energy Fields of the manifested Jinn the Archons the Enitites of Demons and Devils of the Fallen Angel Royals and World Leaders.

You can also get and wear on a neckless with a Lanyard card stating you are exempt from a mask for medical reasons, this will eleviate and relieve any stress while out in daily life conducting your normal life routines of shopping and business, as most of the public you are dealing in are so programmed indoctrinated and brainwashed, they don't even know the true reality of Law and not when it comes to medical grounds, as even a illegitimate unlawful Statute Law enforcing police officer knows they would be breaking two laws if they ask you your medical conditions.

6

BASICS OF COMMON LAW

So why is NATURAL LAW in existence
it is to keep in a permanent state of
validity and to preserve the equality and
equity among and between people and
maintain the natural peace, and this
Universal Natural Law is to guard and
protect the world citizens the people
against tyrannical unjustice governance
and rule by criminal and illegitimate
royals, bloodlines, false rulers.

Common Law ia a comprehensive and
fundamental law, doctrine, or assumption.
Principles so a way of conduct that
everyone should be treated as equals, so
all world citizens should be treated
equally.
All life and things are in existence, living,
life, alive, animated, of therefore of our
physical reality and are held in common,
by the universal state of nature, not one

person has any more of a claim to the planet Gaia, Mother Earth, Pachamama than another person.

So therefore all sentient eternal light beings manifesting in a biological human avatar body, as a man or woman or child on this planet Gaia our Mother Earth, that in this natural manifested physical state all humanities citizens have Equal Rights unto all life and things.

In ancient times the tribal peoples and there communities from all the continents of the planet Gaia our Mother Earth, Pachamama, this Law was commonly known as Customary Law that was the Law of the Land, that applied to and that was for Eternal Spiritual Light Beings manifesting in Human Avatars, to have a human experience and gain spiritual growth.

As stated in the ten commandments and therefore The Creators Law we are to do no harm to others like it says, thy shall not harm ones neighbour, meaning this is a fundamental principle of Common Law. So liberty consists in the freedom to do everything necessary to which harms and injures no one else, we have the right to exercise the rights of each man, woman, or child and these rights have No Limits except those which assure that the other members of humanities society can exercise and enjoy the same equal rights, the only limits on these laws can only be determined by Law.

The only time assessable when the only purpose for which power can be rightfully exercised over another member of society in a civilized community, against a society member, so that individual person of a living breathing man, woman, or child, that can be against that beings wishes, against there will is when it is to prevent harm to others in society.

It is absolute the comprehensive and absolute fundamental law of divine creation that every single child that is birthed is endowed with unalienable liberties that no law, government, religion, absolute no authority that can do away with, diminish or abolish.

Any police officer or person or group, entity or entities, companies or corporation, or false sovereignty bloodlines, that uses any power that tries to encroach or attempts to do tyrannical and illegal therefore illegitimate unlawful crimes of Corporate Statute Law, Law of Contracts birthed from Admiralty Law, Maritime Law, Law of the Sea, which is illegitimate unlawful and criminal, therefore illegal, even if they are working in their own guide lines of their own said laws, for there all can see that there can be no illusion or denial that this is tyranny of evil intentions, so from forces of negative entities and this is an attack, an actual war upon humanity and Divinity its self, an attack on eternal divine angel light beings from the kingdom of light manifesting in as human beings to uplift, inform, illuminate and help free humanity from the negative forces the entities the JINN the ARCHONS, Draco, Demonic Satanic Royal bloodlines with the energy of lucifer.

7

COMMON LAW COURTS
INTENTION

The intention of Common Law Court is determination and resolution, to resolve or intend disputes between eternal embodied beings manifested in human biological avatar bodies as a living breathing man, woman, or child.
The people so all worldwide citizens on planet Gaia our Mother Earth are continually plagued by the injustice of the courts, acting and enforcing illegitimate unlawful criminal Corporate Statute Law, the Law of Contracts, coming from, so birthed from illegal Admiralty Law, the people are also plagued by the injustice of Corporate Statute Law criminal enforcing police officers commiting crimes daily on humanities worldwide citizens as well as other enforcing officers from the tiers of government.

We as natural law citizens under Law of the Land, so under Natural Law, so under a Common Law based judicial system, have the right to associate and gather together in our local communities and can commence and convene a Common Law Court in the capacity of a lawful and legal and just capacity which is of absolute lawful legitimacy, for the people by the people. We are fully and absolutally capable of judging and sentencing any person, organization, company or business fairly regardless of the said status that they hold in society, so this means when a Common Law court is commenced and convened randomly by the citizens they can be trusted to judge fairly with no other alterior motives, We swear into office local community citizens as peace officers who are sworn agents of the court that are directed by our Common Law Court appointed sheriff-officer the appointed civil law enforcement officer, these sworn community citizens are to enforce the sentences of the peoples Common Law Court.

Time ago before there were crowns and Sovereignty governance rulers that were in contract with the people, that then over time gained influence or sway over the people, mainly by manipulation, deception, trickery, with and by there knavish ways, of dishonesty, a lack of integrity that cheat and defraud, deceive and betray the people. So time ago men and women always established their own laws and customs and also established laws between themselves to make certain and ensure that their liberties, their peace were to be free and that they be self governing citizens, self governing people, this is because they were conscious enough to realise that, no one has any right to suppress to control or dominate or rule over another person or persons collectively, or no right to vest ownership to more of creation from another, so cannot own any part of the planet, which is given equally to all world citizens that are eternal spiritual light beings of ultra violet divine energetic consciousness that have manifested into human biological avatar bodies on this said planet Gaia in the present now.

This is because they the people back then were more connected to nature this connected them spiritually and so they recognized Divine Law which is Natural Law of Equality.

First we must start by establishing absolute functioning of Common Law Courts with full jurisdiction over our lives and that of humanities communities at the local levels of our society, so as we take advantage of our natural birthed common law rights and implement them and rely on them daily in all aspects of our lives.

8

THE MAIFESTATION OF COMMON LAW & CIVIL LAW

In the past this came to be and manifested in England after the Luciferian Royals and their elites gained their power of authority over the citizens the people by way of unlawful violent warfare that were not natural in Law or in harmony with nature with life its self, but actually Satanic in nature, with there rape and pillaging of the beautiful wonderful being Mother Earth, Pachamama, of her resources and genocide of humanity.
This is against the basic principles of Divine Law and the basis of equality and peace, and against the peoples WILL, therefore with NO CONSENT.
The Romans power and control of its dominion its realm of supremacy then created their Roman Law legal system known as Civil law that illegitimately criminally decided that the citizens of the

lands the people of men and women did not have the capacity to govern themselves under their own knowledge, wisdom and self rule. The criminal Roman church believes that under the Pope are the people, the chattel, the serves, the subjects, so this means that the authority of all Law is made up invented and composed of illegitimate unlawful statues created by a Sovereign Ruler or a monarch or a Pope or a government this Statute Law derived from Roman Property Law, the law of possessions meaning human beings were devoid of inherent constitutional and natural liberties and so perceived by them to be their serves, their slaves, their possesions of chattel having only prescribed and controlled limited freedoms which are described, characterized and specifically prescribed and formalized by the Sovereignty Monarch Ruler, this lead to a slave system with some having slave advantages, benefits, privileges with more freedom given by favor.

The earlist original corporation on planet Gaia our mother Earth, Pachamama, was the church of Rome this allowed the royals and popes to abolish their responsibilities and dissolve any individual liability, this allows these illegal illigitimate unlawful criminal tyrannical rulers to suppress, dominate, control through fear and debt, criminal activities and have mercilessly gone to war to genocide humanity for thousands of years, but the last six thousand years they have savagely genocided humanity on every continent. So the church of Rome from their centre of operations the Vatican where they weild their power of control to gain profit of commerce, they destroy the planet for resources for profit and ignore even dissolve people liberties world wide. For humanity to get back on track to its divine original plan, we have to set up new governance under Common Law Jurisdiction so under Natural Law Jurisdiction, this will give birth to the new Natural Law authority between humanities worldwide freed peoples with the fundamental purpose of the common courts now needed to selve govern in local communities and this wil dissolve and expel from existence the Roman criminal illegal Civil Law its satanic institutions and dissole all of its past and present authorities.

9

THE COME BACK OF COMMON LAW

On this said planet Gaia our Mother Earth, Pachamama every child birthed is free by its nature and is equal to all and a sovereign of themselves and has the ability and wisdom and the essential Natural Law and Constitutional Law knowledge of what is right and true. So all children, men and women are equal under Law of the Land which is Natural Law, Universal Law. There are other Universal Laws that apply also such as the Law of Divine Oneness, Karmic Law, Law of Attraction are the most popular in society today, (I've listed twelve Universal Laws at the back of this book). All life by its true nature is indivisible it cannot be separated into parts, it is incapable of being divided, so therefore is placed in a common goal for survival and the contemtment of a state of satisfaction, an ease of mind and happiness at the core of there being. So this means then that our personal sovereignty is a mirror of Natural Law, for we are animated living, breathing therefore created and manifested into the physical by Natural Law, Law of the Land which is Universal Law. In all societies this Natural Common Law commonality endows all citizens the people with unalienable rights to establish between themselves their preferred governance and with the unalienable right to protect and defend themselves from treatment of violence and tyranny of others including external authorities. These false criminal royal and Statute Corporate Laws are illegitimate, unlawful, so therefore can be over thrown for there expeditiously and mercilessly unjust genocidal rule at this time in the present now.

The Sovereignty of children, men, and women that have from birth inherent liberties that come from Natural Law which then manifested and created

Common Law, Law of the Land this is so every child, man and woman can defend and protect these divine liberties and live in governed by themselves communities by keeping peace amongst themselves and by cultivating equity for all, free from bias or favoritism. The power of Common Law the authority comes from the people and from the clarity of capacity of the people to determine what is right what is just and to judge right from wrong for themselves, in Common Law courts and its authority alone the twelve people chosen for the jury system will ultimately judge by expression of and in the capacity of Common Law which is Natural Law.

It must also be noted that in Common Law Courts there are no permanent caste members of judges, lawyers as the peoples court has selected and elected temporary sworn in Court officers.

So you can perceive Common Law the Law of the Land which is Natural Law is returning at a swift pace globally to defend and protect world citizens, the worlds peoples from this tyrannical criminal genocidal war on humanity by the Fallen Angel Disgraced Royal Descendants and there co-conspiritors. There plans to submit by force and conquer humanity WILL NOT STAND the Divine plan can be put back on track with the use of Common Law, Natural Law and then humanity can restore the planet Gaia our Mother Earth, Pachamama and humanity back to a balanced equilibrium, with nature and spirit, with the essence of the eternal co-creative collective consciousness of humanity.

Ancient scripture with many predictions that humanity will be released from tyranny of oppressions and all its divisions and that humanity will be restituted back to their natural equality to live and create in harmony with nature and with each other, recognizing the eternal spirit beings that we truly be and that of all realities in the creation.

SUBJECTS FOR CONSIDERATION UNDER COMMON LAW IN COMMON LAW COURTS

Criminal Law and Civil Law are the two main catagories in past established customary patterns that arised from the European continent, so Criminal Law deals with the intentional infliction of harm to another individual person, the truth be known it is when a citizen intentionally inflicts harm to one person they are harming all citizens, it is an offense to the collective of that local community. Civil Law is the dealings of disputes between individual citizens which are considered issues of negligence which have caused harm, this is also known as Tort Offenses.

So civil affairs are settled in Common Law Courts with a jury system in front of our community members, collegues, neighbours and friends.

USING COMMON LAW

Common Law is the basis of how the peoples communities work together in a cohesive collective way to up hold the well being and dignity of all children, men and women of human society, so all citizens on a day to day basis rely and use Common Law when working, socializing and living together, it is simply a way for the citizens the people to organize their daily affairs between one another, it is the constitutional and essential way of nature, so this means existing, living, breathing, animated from nature and permanent as it is an inseparable element associated with the Cosmos of creation and with Divine Eternal Light Beings manifesting into Human Biological Avatar Bodies. This basis is an absolute fundamental nessecity with tyrannical beings that wish to suppress and overthrow the foundations of humanity and that of society and to steal humanities voice of reason and righteousness and that of humanities freedoms.

So Common Law which is Natural Law so Universal Law is needed to stand up to tyrant criminal rulers, governments, corporations, and religion that suppress, deceive to abate and decrease the peoples freedoms, Common Laws solid grounded foundations allow and assures this particular outcome with guaranteed assurances of reciprocated respect and dignity and that of security and protection from the expression of intentional evil from the tyrant rulers that causes mental, emotional, psychological, physical injury, harm, damage to the world citizens the people. These criminal tyrant illegitimate rulers always try to put there authority of statues, so Statute Laws above that of Constitutional Law, Common Law which is Natural Law so Universal Law to suppress control dominate and enslave communities of humanity.

The fact that Common Law is the reigning Supreme Law of the mass populace of humanity, it means only a small percentage of humanities citizens need to set up Common Law courts and practice Common Law for the criminal corporation, criminal Statute Law system of illegitimate unlawful illegal contracts to collapse, disintergrate and become non-existant. So humanity the people need to push back with the peoples Sovereignty of Common Law in all communities worldwide to protect all areas and aspects of our daily lives, against unreasonable characteristic evil behaviors from these rulers of statues, rulers of criminal and unlawful Statute Law.

Common Law manifested from the encroachment of an unchecked illegitimate sovereignty ruler from bloodlines of tyrants that suppress, rape, pillage, force excessive taxs upon the citizens the people. Common Law conventionally has negotiated and handled Criminal Law issues that the religious church institutions Canon Law court system and the Sovereignty rulers Crown Law Court system, are unwilling to accept absolutely, but some cases they will hear in a confined and controlled way, with crimes that occur to the community even crimes commited of rape, murder and the violence of the crime warfare and genocide.

The absolute universal jurisdiction of the legal matters in communities under Common Law courts which are under Natural Law, Universal Law is needed to deal with individual personal civil affairs during engaging arguments and disputes within the communities.

In Common Law Courts in Criminal Law litigation affairs, just as in any other lawful system of law, the burden of proof in such litigation brought infront of the Common Law Courts will be on the ones who bring the lawsuit to bare they are the plaintiffs, and the standard rules of evidence will be implemented and administered, such as if provable facts must be shown to the court like original certified documentation that's has been clarified by an independent party, also by living breathing witnesses that saw when the alleged crime occurred, this is the basis of truthful provable facts that are needed to even bring allegations against another person, persons, party or parties. When it comes to the charge of serious crimes such as rape, murder, genocide the most important rule is that there cannot be under any cirumstances absolutely No Hear say Evidence allowed, it is essential and critical as it is inadmissibile as a rule of evidence.

If any allegations are made by a plaintiff they must prove the the one(s) accused were seen by an eyewitness in the act of the alleged crime or it must be shown to the court that they were direct participants in the alleged crime with truthful provable evidence of facts.

12

COMMON LAW JURIES OVER JUDGES LEADS TO A FAIR JUDGEMENT

This solves much of the problem of corruption from one self governing judge and any manipulation and blackmail by politians or outside influence, where as with a group of jurors the rule of evidence has a definite better assurance against abuse and corruption this allows a swift and just conduct in the Common Court processes. This is especially evident when a self governing judge has to rule against his peers, collegues and employers that of the government and illegitimate Sovereignty rulers there is not any confidence in there ability or in their jurisdictional duties to rule against their criminal employers. This is known to happen in Statute Law that evidence is removed and destroyed or simply altered in some fashion to favour the desired party, or waived, its also known that the Legal Due Process is not followed and ignored, some judges even silencing one particular party in a dispute, this is criminal, unlawful and illegal. Usually protecting and covering up the sickest horrific disturbing crimes of rulers there governance employees, elite circles especially involving child crimes, pedophilia, rape, murder, human trafficking, drug smuggling, gun running and terrorist affiliations.

This is how you stop and prevent corruption, manipulation of the justice of law by creating and establishing a Common Law Court that's run by the people, run by the jury, this stops vested interests corrupting the Common Law Court of Justice system.

13

FOUNDING CONSTITUTING & PRESERVING OUR COMMON LAW COURTS

The first thing is defined clear principles are needed to be put in place to validate the Common Law Courts lawfulness and its legitimacy for the people by the people, then the Common Law Courts have powers that are legitimate to protect the people individual or as a collective community, then able to use that power to indict and prosecute entities such as corporations, establishments or entity a single person that are unpropitious to the community acting in the manners of being menacing, intimidating, abusive and terrorizing, and to charge them with a crime or crimes by finding or presentment of a grand jury in Common Law Courts.

The Peoples command the Peoples authorization to establish Common Law

Courts is obtained from and by the Sovereignty of the people as a collective, from there Unalienable birth Rights being that we are Eternal Immortal Interdimensional Light Beings of Divine Ultra Violet Energetic Consciousness, from the eternal Kingdom of Light outside time and space, we are a part of the Whole Brahaman's, the Whole Creations collective consciousness, Manifesting into Divine human biological avatar bodies.

It is a cosmic universal fact that Common Law Courts with its universal jurisdiction that comes from Natural Law, this means that Common Law Courts can be set up and established in any Nation, Country, Community on any Planet in and through out the Universe. This is because Common Law Courts universally are not constricted by old paradigm illusionary laws or traditional boarders, and they do not recognize any other privileges, immunity or legal or moral authority, and they are able to absolutely handle to manage and conduct with confidence and jurisdictionally competency to judge to adjudicate all grievances or issues.

When a community has matters of concern and congrigate what ever the number of women and men that are gathered a Common Law Court can be created and therefore recognized as legitimate as its constituted by the Sovereignty of the People.
Common Law courts are the manifestation and clear expression and so the Voice of the People, that can then gather and communicate there demands and concerns and therefore are perceived as committees of the people considering or acting on community affairs that are councils of conscience.
It is the vote of the People as a collective with there absolute explicit Divine will that the Common Law Court is established, then they must choose and elect twelve community members of the people as the Citizen Jury, they must also choose and elect a Presiding Adjudicator but their job is strictly advisory, then a

Citizen Prosecutor is selected to conduct the case on behalf of the people, then a Sheriff-officer and a group of Peace officers which are needed to enforce warrants, summons and verdicts of the Common Law courts.

The communities peoples can also appoint Justices of the Peace known also as Local Magistrates, they have the peoples power to start and initiate the formation of a Common Law Court and they have the peoples power to summons juries and issue warrants.

Under the Common Law Court system it applies to both the defendants and the plaintiffs that are concerned in affairs before the court that they must represent, so present their own cases in all of the court preceedings, this is because if you allow another to represent on your behalf it means that you are constituting a surrender of your Natural Rights and Sovereignty.

In a Common Law Court there are no constraints of the Rights of the court or any time frame of limitation on its duration, they have full unrestricted power to access any thing or place or person. The Common Law Court can along with the elected magistrates can issue public summons that are legally binding on any corporation, company, institution, persons or person, that will be enforced by the Common Courts Sheriff-officer who has full authority of the court from the people to detain any person that is named in the summons and return them physically to the Common Law Court. When a Common Law Courts jury has reached a verdict it cannot be appealed its decision is final, this is because sound minded citizens knowing truth from lie and right from wrong with a moral truthful basis and with the evidence alone, concluded with reason and no coercion to the said verdict, for the truth is not subject to revision or reconsideration, because if reconsidered then it was not of the original truth, it was simply not true of the original context. But if it can be unlawfully founded and proven beyond a doubt that there was any unduly influence or faulty evidence the case of affairs can be reopened by the Magistrate and retried with Common Law Court officers and a jury present, also the decision sentence of the court is final and then is enforced by the appointed Common Law Court sheriff-officer by the power of the people he has bestowed upon him by the people and the people can help and assist him enforce his duty if required to do so. This is because the citizens the people of the community have direct responsibility of all of the procedures of the Common Law Court and responsibility of the community citizens, this governing of democratic laws and decisions is a verdict of the peoples declaration to govern themselves. The citizen jury has no constraints of there power to officially force a ruling a sentence on to any corporation, company, institution, persons or person, it must also be said that the Magistrate or the Common Law Courts Adjudicator has absolute no power to change by direction, or influence or alter the juries original sentence verdict of the original jury, the Magistrate or the Adjudicator are only allowed to communicate to the jury the matters of the points of the legal procedure of the Law. The Common Law Court jury citizens are liberated from there duties only when the final sentence decision is reached upon and the verdict final. It is the people that participate and give arise to the Common Law Court and it is there sworn duty to maintain it with their Eternal Divine Conscious Consent.

14

THE COMMON LAW COURTS PROTOCOL AND LEGAL PROCEDURES

Universal law which is Natural Law so then Common Law, its foundation of legal methods of procedures and practices are based on the centrality of Due Process that are to have the right to be informed and notified of any charges that have been brought against them, and to see all the evidence brought against them in a suit, also for them to be judged and tried infront of their own peers the communities citizens the people, their neighbours. If a person who is acussed is not given these three rights and given the chance to freely defend themselves in the Common Law Court, then this means that no legitimate trial can proceed and no conviction can be carried out as there can be no conclusion rendered.

The three main said Rights of Common Law Courts as based on the essential fundamental beliefs concepted of the Common Law doctrines, that are –

A – It is always absolutely presumed that the said accused is innocent and not guilty.

B – That the burden of proof of the said indicted accused's guilt rests upon the defendant but it is the plaintiff who must absolutely concvince a jury of the guilt of the accused absolutely completely beyond any reasonable doubt.

C – Also the said accused cannot be held and detained with out the process of due process, but must always appear expeditiously in a speedy and timely manner before the Common Law Court by physical appearance before the court.

To stop proceedings being drawn out or impeded to the due process and to justice itself, the Common Law Court sets out strict time limits on the pretrial proceedings after which a trial must ensue and commence but not before both sides of the dispute have been given equal amounts of time to file their evidence and statements and allowed to make their motions to the Common Law Court and able to respond to any said accusations and arguments.

So before there is even any Common Law Court appearance the procedure is designed to have a pretrial period where both sides are given their liberties, there rights to give their presentation of evidence and their course of arguments to each other of the both parties in the disputed affairs, this is to try to reach and seek a settlement before any court apperances. This procedure of presenting ones case is known as To See and To Say or referenced as the Examination for Discovery, this is where either of the both parties can request to see and demand any documentation or relevant evidence from the other said parties. If there can be no settlement between the said parties then a trial will be set by the Common Law Court convening and set a time and date for the trial to start and commence.

15

THE PROTOCOLS TO BE FOLLOWED BY ANYONE SEEKING TO ACCUSE ANOTHER & TRY OTHER PARTIES IN COMMON LAW COURT

The first Protocol of procedure is to have a Statement of Claim that must be produced by those bringing a case to the Common Law Court that are the Plaintiffs, this means their basically summarising the significant information of there statement about the actual facts of the case of their said disputes, by a remedy being sought after for the wrongs of bad, immoral or unjust such things being alleged by the plaintiff this maybe be relieved by a remedy of agreed terms by both said parties.

Then the Plaintiffs Statement of claim must be followed up with supporting evidence of testimonies and documents that will be used in proving their case absolutely beyond any reasonable doubt, the evidence must always be sworn in by anyone who is not a party to the said dispute in the form of the original documents themselves only, and in the form of witnessed statements, which must testify in the Common Law Court physically in person to affirm and testify to their own statement.

The second Protocol of procedure is to file a Notice of Claim of Right in the Common Law Court to achieve redress to set right and remedy the said affairs of discord their lack of agreement. The plaintiff after collection of evidence and assembling their case must then obtain the support of the Common Law Officers and that of the Common Law Court, there must be a publishing of a Notice of Claim of Right, in well known public locations of importance, and normally in specific buildings like the library or town hall and pulished in the local new papers, so a court can be created and brought into being, this is a declaration publically openly in a public manner asking and calling on assistance from the citizens of the community to assert the Plaintiffs right under Natural Law for the intention of Natural Justice, by having a jury of their peers, neighbours hear there case through and under Common Law which is Natural Law and so therefore is Universal Law.

The third Protocol of procedure is the creation and the assembling of the Common Law Court, this must occur after the Notice of Claim of Right has been circulated and must occur within twenty four hours of the Notice being made public to the community, then the procedure next is to constitute any twelve citizens of the community, anyone can be considered to constitute themselves as a Common Law Court and its composed formed jury, then following this they must appoint the Court officers from their selected commity, one being a citizen prosecutor or a public prosecutor to direct the course of the case this is usually the

Plaintiff themselves or a person they authorizes to advise them only, in no way to represent them on there behalf. Two a Court Adjudicator must be appointed to advise the Common Court appointed citizens of the community and to over see the court proceedings in its entirety. Three is to appoint a Defense Counsel to advise only, but not in any way represent the accused. Four is to appoint the Court Sheriff-officer from the community or from authorized delegated existing Peace officers. Five is to appoint the Bailiffs which are the Court reporter and the important Court Registrar.

It is expected that these procedures will be carried out in the correct fashion and manner by the citizens the people that are appointed into or creating the Common Law Court and that they act in the capacities of the Knowledge of the Common Law which is Natural Law that's Universal Law.

The fourth Protocol of procedure is the Oath of office and the swearing in of the

Court officers and the jury of twelve citizens, and then convening to start proceedings of the Common Law Court. Next the Adjudicator which is the Magistrate or the Justice of Peace they will formally start and convene and assemble the Court by taking and then administering the Oath of Common Law Court Office to all of the Court officers.

THE OATH OF COMMON LAW COURT OFFICE

I (Individuals Name) swear I will truthfully and faithfully perform my obligated duties as an officer of this Common Law Court according to the principles of Natural Justice and the principles of Due Proccess, behaving and acting at all times with lawfulness, honesty and integrity.

I also recognize that if I fail to do so, to consistently abide by this said Oath I can and will be removed from my Office, of the Common Law Court.

I make this statement of the public Oath freely with clarity and without mental reservation with no uncertainty or ulterior motive or coercion.

Subsequently after pledging the Oath, the then Baliffs, Sheriff-officers, jury members, court counsellors and the reporter will then assemble and receive instructions from the Adjudicator concerning the said case. The Adjudicator is the Advisor to the Court they are not presiding Magistrates or Judges, they can not halt any actions or the decisions of the Jury or other Court officers they do not have the power to influence and cannot direct actions, the only time the Adjudicator can step in is when negligence or a gross miscarriage of justice has occured by the other Court officers. This type of self governance means the Court is dependant and self regulating on the understanding of the mutual respect and truthful governance of all of the said Common Law Court Jury and that of the Common Law Court other officers.

The fifth Protocol of proceedure is the Pretrial Conference to try to achieve a settlement before, to avoid a trial, both parties are brought together by the Adjudicator to then Examine both of each parties mandatory Examination of Discovery, this is where statements, counter evidence and evidence from both parties will be presented, the trial conferences time frame is up to a week then will end, then if there is no resolution between the parties a trial will have to begin and commence.

The sixth Protocol of procedure is then the circulating and issuing of Public Summonses, no agency or persons or person can be lawfully summoned into a Common Law Court without first getting and receiving the Complete Set of Charges being brought against them by the Plainitiff, they must also receive the legitimate formal Notice to Appear before

the Common Law Court or a Writ of
Public Summons, the summons must be
clearly laid out with the correct trial start
date, time and address of venue of the
Common Law Court.
When a summons is needed to be issued
the Plaintiff must apply for this through
the Court Registrar, then the summons
can be issued under the signature of the
Court Adjudicator and then will be
dispatched to the Defendant by the Court
Sheriff-officer, this must be done within
twenty four hours, so one day of its initial
Filing in the Court Registry by the
Plaintiff, the Sheriff-officer is personally
responsible to deliver and serve the
Defendant, also if the Defendant avoids
service which they have a week to appear
before the Common Law Court from the
date of service, then the Sheriff-officer
would post the summons from a public
space that is recorded.

The seventh Protocol of procedure is the
Trial is initiated and commences starting
with Statements of the Opening

Arguments, the Adjudicator starts with an introduction and then the Opening Arguments are presented first by the plaintiff or it maybe a Procecutor, and then the Defendant will present case, the two Counsilers and the Adjudicator will then have the opportunity to question both parties for there clarification and then able to make motions to the Common Law Court if it is at all apparent that the whole proceedings can be expedited. Protocol seven can and will be conducted even if the plaintiff or Defendant is not physically present in person in the Common Law Court as some individuals or entities may refuse to participate, this type of trial in commence is called In Absentia and is known to be legal and legitimate in procedure but the Defendant must have the opportunity to respond and appear to the evidence and charges against them, a trial like this is started by the Plaintiffs Opening Argument presentation followed by there central case, with an absent Defendant the Common Law Court Appointed Defense

Counsel will be given the opportunity to argue the Defendants case, if this is the wishes of the Defendant.

In many cases there are no responses or appearences from the Defendant which the Adjudicator advising the Jury to declare a verdict in the favour of the Plaintiff, this would be on the grounds that the Defendant has silently agreed with the case against them, this is because they do not dispute the charges or the evidence against them, and they made no attempt to appear in the Common Law Court and try to defend themselves and their own name in public, to the sworn in citizen officers or to the community peoples present, in Common Law Court.

The eighth Protocol of procedure is the opening and commence of the main proceedings and assuming everyone of all parties are present in the Common Law Court, then starting with the Plaintiff giving their presentation of evidence and there argument against the said Defendant, who will get the opportunity to respond, the Citizen Prosecutor may assist the Plaintiff if need be. Once the Plaintiff has presented there case the Defendant or his advising Counsel can then cross examine the Plaintiff, then after this the Defendant will present their case on there own or with an advising Counselor and then in turn will be cross examined by the Plaintiff or by the Citizen Prosecutor.

The ninth Protocol of procedure is the final advice of the Adjudicator in the closing arguments to the jury, the Adjudicator after the main proceedings have occurred can ask additional questions to both parties so they can give the final advice to the Jury in session, then both the Defendant and the Plaintiff can give there closing statement summary and argument to the Common Law Court, then the closing by the Adjudicator with any final remarks to the Jury.

The tenth Protocol of procedure is that the Jury will withdraw to deliberate at this time the Common Law Court will be held in recess, this will allow the twelve citizen jurors to come to a unanimous verdict and a sentence that is based on their appraisal of all the evidence in full, the deliberations have no time frame with no restristions, at this time the Jury may have no contact with anyone but the Court Balliff who is their Guard and Escort, the sentence and verdict by the Jury must always be non-coerced, consensual and unanimous in conclusion.

The eleventh Protocol of procedure is a unanimous decision of sentence and the verdict is issued by the Jury, the Common Law Court will reassemble when the verdict is reached by the Jury but if the jurors are not in agreement and are not in accord concerning the verdict, then the Defendant will be consequently declared innocent, the agreed upon spokesperson for the Jury declares the verdict to the Common law Court and the said sentence that is based on that particular verdict will also be divulged by the Jury spokesperson.

 The twelfth Proctocol of procedure is when the Common Law Court is Adjourned and the Juries sentence is to be Enforced, once the final verdict and sentence is declared to the Court the Adjudicator will free the Defendant or authorizes the Juries decision in the name of the community and there Common Law Court, and then notify the Sheriff-officer to enforce the said sentence. The Adjudicator will conclude the trial proceedings and disband the Jury and close the Court session. The Adjudicator or any other parties cannot in any way compromise, alter or withhold any of the Records of the Trial Court Proceedings they are accessible to any citizen and are classified as Public Documents.

16

THE COMMON LAW LEGAL FORM OF THE OATH OF THE COMMON LAW COURT OFFICE & TWO DOCUMENTATION FORMS OF NOTICE & WARRANT TO DEPUTIZE & NOTICES OF CLAIM OF RIGHT NOTICE

The OATH of Common Law Court Office

To be disseminated and issued to any citizen of the community that is sworn in as an agent of the Common Law Court or to any law enforcement officers that are deputized by the Common Law Court Office or issued by the Common Law Courts Sheriff-officers.

The declaration model form is below –

I, ___FULL NAME___, being of sound mind and of clear conscience, do hereby swear that I will absolutely truthfully and faithfully and justly perform and execute the office of an agent of the Common Law Court of Justice according to the absolute best of my abilities.

I understand that if I fail in my sworn duties or I am compromised or betray the trust and responsibilities of my office of the Common Law Court I will automatically forfeit my right to this position and can be dismissed immediately.

I take this serious and dignified solemn OATH freely with no reservations, with no ulterior motive and without coercion, according to my conscience as a free man or woman, and as a citizen under the authority and jurisdiction of the Common Law.

_____ Signature, SIGNED

_____ Date

_____ Common Law Court
Offical Stamp.

THE NOTICE & WARRANT TO
DEPUTIZE that is issued UNDER the
AUTHORITY of the SHERIFF-Officers
Office of the COMMON LAW COURT
of JUSTICE and under the
JURISDICTION of NATURAL LAW &
the LAW of NATIONS.

To all Peace Officers & all Officials of
Law & Enforcement Officers of Statute
Law –

This Public Notice is issued to you as a
lawful warrant by the Common Law
Court of Justice, placing you under the
jurisdiction of the Common Law Court
and Natural Justice, and deputizing you
as its Official Peace Officers.

Upon your taking of the official appended sworn OATH of Common Law Court Office, you are empowered to act as the lawful agents and protectors of the Common Law Court and all its proceedings, and are sworn to serve and enforce its, Warrants, Writs, Summons and Courts Orders on any and all Persons and Institutions, Corporations, companies named by the Common Law Court.

If you choose not to take this OATH of office to the Common Law Court Office, you are compelled and Ordered by the Common Law Court and by Natural Law to refrain from interfering with the actions of the Sheriff-Officer or other Peace Officers that are deputized and are legitimately & fully empowered to act for the Common Law Court of Justice.

If you resist, impede or disrupt the actions of the Common Law Court Orders or its Sworn Sheriff-officers or Peace Officers you can and will be CHARGED with CRIMINAL ASSAULT and OBSTRUCTION of JUSTICE.

Issued on_____ in the community of
_____ by the following Legal Agent
or Sworn Peace Officer or Sheriff-officer
of the Common Law Court of Justice –
_____ Signature, SIGNED
_____ Common Law Courts
Offical Stamp.

PUBLIC NOTICE of CLAIM of RIGHT
to be Publicly issued in order to convene
and assemble a local Common Law
Court.

Issued by ____FULL NAME____ on
____DATE____ in the community of
_____.

I ____FULL NAME____ give Public
Notice of my personal claim of right and
of my lawful excuse to convene and
assemble and establish a Common Law
Court under my liberty as an Eternal

Spirit Light Being embodied as a Human Being, a flesh and blood man or woman, and hereby call upon the support of all competent men and women to assist me in this Lawful Right.

I further give Public Notice of my absolute personal Right of Claim and of my lawful excuse to convene and assemble and establish as part of such a court a jury of my peers, consisting of twelve men or women, to judge a matter of affairs affecting the well being, safety, rights, protection and security of myself and my community, that matter of affairs being of the following – The description of the said issue, also a statement of claim and the named parties.

I further give Public Notice that the said Jury of my peers claims the jurisdictional competence, capability and capacity to judge this matter of affairs and issue a verdict and a sentence within the said Common Law Court assembled and established to render such a judgement, based upon absolute proven and irrefutable evidence presented within its Common Law Court.

I hereby publicly advocate and so call upon and appeal and request the support of my community to assemble and establish this Common Law Court and its Jury of twelve men or women, to be sworn to act in such a capacity for the scope and duration of the Common Law Court proceedings, according to Natural Law and the rules of due process and evidence.

I make this Public Claim of Right freely without ulterior motive or coercion, in the public interest of Justice and in the interest of the Publics and the Communities Welfare.

_____ Claimant Signature

_____ Witness   Signature

_____ Date.

17

THE ENFORCEMENT OF COMMON LAW

All able bodied citizens of the community are obligated, obliged and Sovereignty empowered by Natural Law to support and assist the Common Law Courts Sheriff-officer and their Deputy-officers to enforce the sentence of the Common Law Court by securing the imprisonment of the guilty, and by assisting in the vigilant surveillance and monitoring of his associates and assist in the seizure of property or assets of the guilty party and his associated agents, if this is the will of the Common Law Courts decision, this is really for the safety of the community that the collective of Law Enforcement may be required if the guilty party or the head said officers of that entity or body or an entire corporation or institution, may be of many persons that is why the Citizens must assist the Common Law

Courts Law enforcement officers, as there is always more safety guaranteed in numbers.

18

IN THE COMMON LAW SYSTEM THE DECISION STANDS AS THE FOUNDATION OF LEGALITY

The principle and position of the knowledge and belief of the policy of following rules of the principles laid out that legal decisions are binding and final and shall not be reversed. When the Common Law Court has entered a judgement the decision that stands upon an issue, it cannot be reversed, the decision stands, this is one of the key differences between Civil Law and Common Law, as the decision that stands with no ability to reverse the decision is actually a fact of the foundation of legality in the Common Law Court system. With the Common Law Courts solidity of a verdict by protocol and procedure and the custom of The Decision Stands, this means verdicts have Binding Authority that have precedent of decisions made in previous Court verdicts, this means that The Decision Stands, custom also stops any interference from illegitimate rulers and there political intrusions, intervention and obstruction.

19

THE APPEALING OF COMMON LAW COURT DECISIONS

Natural Law principles states that every child, man and women are born with the existing natural permanent qualities that understand right from wrong and that of justice, so this means when a Jury of the communities twelve citizens deliberate after both parties in the argued dispute, in a case, having given the complete facts and evidence of the case, will be able to arrive at a proper and just verdict. The verdicts of the Common Law Jury therefore are not subject to revision or appeal because the truth is not capable of being reformed and the truth is not mutable and therefore cannot be changed as the truth is the constant fact of Nature. There can be no evaluation of the truth of the verdict given it can only be disputed if it is found there was no proper examination of evidence or if there was a gross dereliction of duty.

20

THE CONVICTING OF ILLEGITIMATE RULERS & THEIR INSTITUTIONS BY WAY OF VERDICTS & ENFORCING THOSE VERDICTS

All worldwide legal systems are conducted by there view of the world around them and by there relation to and constituting essence of there essential purpose, in the circumstances and conditions of Statute Law or Civil Law, the goal of the process of the Court is to determine the most truthful and convincing argument as they spar in the Courtroom between the two parties that are in dispute over particular affairs or incident of the said case. The Magistrate who is constituted and comprised from an unaccountable small judicial exclusive group that are self governing, usually a sole Magistrate in this Court system will hear both parties but is favourable and serves the party that has the most influence or and money to present the most convincing presentation of there said case.

This type of illegitimate Law Statute Law or Civil Law is not used for the common good of citizens and communities it is actually used as a privy weapon to use, apply, weild, operate, manipulate and brandish against a member of the community one of the people or peoples a group over commercial interests, this illegitimate Law systems origin comes from the Illegitimate Unlawful Criminal False Sovereignty Rulers and there corrupt elite governace minions.

But contrarily in the Common Law Courts by Common Law the needs of the community as a collective is outlined and defined, not contending to individual interests and outlined is those from the community that have had an inadequacy and shortcomings of justice, Common Law conducts it procedures from the base of morality this is how it forms and where it manifested and formed from, the Injustices of Intentional Inherent Evil from Illegitimate Rulers. So Common Law acts and operates from this very simple basis that with any legal decision taken by the Common Law Court or any precedent taken, it will serve the collective community as a whole, and the Common Law Courts decision will best serve the ones in the community who have been victimized, those that have suffered or those thay may be vunerable in the future.

Naturally under their conscious cognitive conversing, men and women have the full capability and capacity to mediates their own affairs and disputes among themselves and have the natural tendency to resolve and conclude from the basic principles of Common Law which is knowing right from wrong.

However we can see external authoritive forces through extreme and violent means threaten and force the community and the so the people by conditioning of deceit and trickery by way of words and use of grammer of language to entrap you into a verbal contract, that is illegitimate and unlawful from Statute Law, the Law of Contracts deriving from Admiralty Law which is Maritime Law also known as Law of the Sea which is illegitimate on this planet Gaia our Mother Earth, Pachamama, for the Law that stands on this planet is Law of the Land which is Common Law that is Natural Law that is Universal Law, Law of the Universe. This continuum of threats and violence of force from illegitimate Rulers and there State and Governance that try to deny the community and its citizens the Sovereign People from there own judgements and try to get the people to put off, defer to the illegitimate external authorities when they seek justice or resolve from a dispute.

21

COMMON LAW RETURNS THE SOVEREIGNTY OF THE PEOPLE COMING BACK INTO POWER

Common Laws daily use is returning and the need for Common Law Courts in our society is returning after much deceit and straight up lies and trickery used by the Illegitimate Statute Law, which is UNLAWFUL therefore carries NO WEIGHT and therefore is INVALID, over the Sovereignty of Spititual Eternal Light Beings manifested in a biological Human Avatar body, Common Law is a nessecary fundamental part of the functional parts of a community, society, civilization and that of the universal galactic collective of of all races and species in the creation of over 200 trillion galaxies, under Natural Law which is under Universal Law.

So Common Law is coming back strong in the face of Genocidal Tyranny and will once again be a part of daily human life, the citizens of communities taking back there UNALIENABLE RIGHTS, from birth under Common Law, the Law of the Land which is Natural Law which is Universal Law. The people seem to be awakening back up to the Sovereignty of themselves and in the governance of all their affairs, Common Law Courts are reappearing around the world as the People start to take back their birth Unalienable Rights, of Universal Natural Common Law with the understanding that there is common curtsies between Eternal Spiritual Beings of Light that are embodied in Human Avatars. Understanding humanity is goverened by Natural Law that is Common Law this come back in our communities will bring efficacy back to the Justice system, but more Common Law Courts need to be opened worldwide to secure The Peoples Sovereignty Powers and Unalienable Rights and of course stem the tyranny of the Illegitimate False Rulers of the Fallen

Angel descendants Royal disgraced despicable despised bloodlines.

When it is time for a communities citizens to perform there said sworn Common Law duties, the biggest hindrance to the process of there capabilities and capacities is if there own doubts and fears arise when having to apprehend, detain and seize the Citizen or Defendant in a warrant served by the Common Law Court of Justice, this could lead to inefficacy and then in turn impede the Common Law Courts proceedings, but with the correct and proper training and interactive hours on the Job this can be avoided. Also it it every citizen of the communities duty to study and know the Common Laws of the Land, it's a duty to self to know ones Sovereignty of self and of there Unalienable Rights of Natural Law and be able to represent the community and be able to be Just and Fair in in there intentions, actions and decisions.

In Common Law the Jury system is a

transparent manifestion of Natural Law with clarity of authentic expression this enables the Power of the People, that can then ascertain the particular truths of affairs in the disputed matters of the community between the citizens the people, it allows them to defend there customs and values and actions within the capacity of Common Law, Law of the Land which is Natural Law and in turn is Universal Law.The Common Law citizen using there amplitude of ability to judge a lawsuit for themselves under Oath as a sworn officer of the Common Law Court as a juror, and so be able to reach a verdict and sentence in said suits.

When the community citizens the people are united to determine the truths of the said affairs in question and can assemble the evidence they will come to a verdict that is of Truthfulness and therefore Just. So if there was no coercion, threats or influence and the evidence and facts were considered collectedly, then the verdict reached will or should be a reasonable and fair out come. So it should be the collective truths and morality of the jurors that invalidates any prejudice or bias from any individual juror(s) for the natural reasons of truths manifested from compassion and equity of fairness and Just, according to Natural Law, so Natural Rights with specific freedom from favouritism and bias, the reality though is there is invariably evident individual prejudice or bais that is in some form is present, this is irrefutable so incontestable.

22

THE ENFORCING OF COMMON LAW COURT VERDICTS ISSUED

This is a key aspect of the Common Law Court the Common Law enforcers the Sheriff-officers and the Peace officers, that are sworn in under Oath to implement there said duties, the Common Law Court cannot operate and function without this key fundamental arm of Peace Enforcers. The customs of the Common Law Sheriff-officer that are community citizens of the People are men and women that are chosen, selected and appointed and delegated to detain those citizens that harm others in the community and to bring them into village, town, county, city courts for judgement to enforce the Common Law Courts verdict sentence.
The acting role of the Common Law Sheriff-officer is –

To provide security for the Common Law Court.

To deliver Common Law Court summons and orders to appear before the Court.

To detain by physically delivering to the Common Law Court those citizens who have been summoned but who have avoided, evaded and circumnavigated a Common Law Court order.

To enforce the absolute final sentence of the Common Law Court this includes the imprisonment in jail and the surveillance and monitering of guilty citizens.

So the Sheriff-officer peforms there duties with the aid of other sworn in Peace officer deputies and other agents he appoints to assist in the duties handed down by the Common Law Court of Justice.

In past times and now current times the Sheriff-officer and his deputies of Peace officers which is the organization and assembling of able bodied men from the community to stop and restrain any citizen from the community or from other

communities that have commited
unlawful crimes, they the Sheriff-officers,
Peace officers and Deputies are to do the
up most in ones power to fulfil there said
sworn duties, they are known as a posse.
The Common Law Court Sheriff-officer
is therefore the servant of the community
the servant of the citizens the People,
sworn in by the citizens the People and so
recallable by the citizens the People and
answerable to citizens of the community,
the People and so the Sheriff-officer is
not above the People or is not an
extraneous outside force over the People.
The tradition of the community electing
and appointing Sheriff-officers and Peace
officers and deputies derived from the
belief that all citizens of a community had
a duty an obligation to protect and police
themselves their kin and especially the
communities children and the vunerable
in the community.
The Authority that is given by the
Common Law Court, so the Authority of
the communities citizens, the people to
the Sheriff-officer allows him the power

to deputize any citizen to assist in there duties, this includes agents, police officers and other citizens that are representing illegitimate Rulers, governments, corporations, companies, institutions that are being Named and Tried in Common Law Courts, this is a vital strategy while the come back and return of Common Law and Common Law Courts on planet Earth are implemented, as this action allows the People to use the fortitude of these illegitimate unlawful institutions and there systems against them, as they are dismantled and replaced, this allows the deputized citizens that work for these unlawful institutions to work with and stand with the People, for the over all benefit and well being of the community as a whole and can also become witnesses to the illegitimate unlawful activities and crimes, and to assist the Sheriff-officer and there Peace officers and Deputies in the apprehending, arresting, and detainment of the accused to be sentenced in the Common Law Court by the People.

This means the peoples voice through the Common Law Court is voiced through the Courts issue of an Arrest Warrant or Summonses on behalf of the community, it is the Common Law Court Sheriff-officer that will first deliver a copy of the said Summons to the pre-existing regional local police agency station, with also the Deputizing Notice this then places those police officers under the Jurisdiction of the Common Law. Then by Law of the Land which is Common Law the police officers that have all already Sworn an Oath to Constitutional Law which is Common Law, are lawfully duty bound obliged and obligated to assist the Common Law Sheriff-officer and there Peace officers in there duties and then the police officers must swear the same Oath that the Sheriff-officer has sworn that of the Common Law Office. It maybe that a police officer or other agents of the arms of the illegitimate unlawful government, that are issued with a Common Law Notice may dispute it or deny it or refuse to recite, to take the

Common Law Oath, if this is the circumstance they must not interfere and will be ordered to stand down from there position, and not to intervene in the Sheriff-officers Common Law duties. It will be assumed that the police officers through them not interfering and through there silence, that they are agreeing with the Common Law Notice, this means these police officers are silently tacitly then abiding by the actual Common Law Notice Action, this will then invalidate the standard protections that these criminals that Rule and that are in high positions of governance and office, in these illegitimate unlawful corporations and institutions.

This will bring moral conflict to the very surface of all levels of our society and to the core of our local communites worldwide, as there will be naturally at first some inevitable moral confrontations and conversing on moral ethics the code that extends beyond the individual to include what is determined to be right and wrong for the community or society as a whole, there will be a conflict between the two legal systems, the Illegitimate Unlawful Corporation Statute Law from Admiralty Law, Law of the Sea and the Lawful Legal Universal Law which is Natural Law which is Common Law, Law of the Land which is Constitutional Law. The worldwide citizens of all communities will perceive this conflict arise in the fabric of society and have to educate themselves on these said Laws and step up to there Natural Law Duties of Common Law, and to protect there citizens in there communities their kin, neigbours, collegues.

23

THE INEVITABLE CONFRONTATION OF ILLEGITIMATE UNLAWFUL CORPORATE STATUTE LAW ENFORCING CIVIL LAW POLICE OFFICERS
AGAINST
THE LAWFUL LEGAL UNIVERSAL LAW - NATURAL LAW - COMMON LAW COURT SHERIFF-OFFICERS & THERE SWORN IN PEACE OFFICERS & DEPUTIES

Humanity is in grave peril at this time negative agendas from evil dark forces rage in a spiritual battle for the control of this planet Gaia and for Humanities absolute enslavement, from tyrannical Rulers and there Masters, but freedom is coming the chains will be cast as humanity awakens to there eternal spirit within, a Consciousness Awakening on all levels of society, life and of their entire being, one being that of the illusions of reality they have been living under. These two conflicting sides of the two Law Systems must be always directly filmed and streamed live to the worldwide citizens to the people, when they are confronting one another as this will ultimately make the police officers and the military officers have to make a decisive decision choosing a side to serve, the illegitimate unlawful criminal rulers and there corporations and institutions or serve the communites serve the People.

We see around the world that when Common Law Court Sheriff-officers have interacted with police officers that they have backed down and have not interfered with the Common Law Court Sheriff-officers duties. As police officers swear an Oath of constitutional Law which is Common Law if they receive a Common Law Court Order they are duty bound to enforce the said Order, and obliged and obligated to arrest the named defendant or defendants on the said Common Law Notice Order.

24

THE PEOPLE
BECOME THE POLICE PEACE
OFFICER AUTHORITIES

Common Law is not just an armory for
the self defense of the communities
citizens, the people the individuals that
are persecuted, suppressed and actually
tyrannized, but also Common Law being
established and implemented will bring
change to the fabric of our society
absolutally, fundamentally, to political
and social change and a complete
transformational shift in the way we
govern ourselfs and our communities.
When the People stand in there Birth
Right Sovereignty Power and become
there own police peace officer authorities
under Common Law the People regain
there power. As the people stand up to the
tyrannical illegitimate corporate Statute
Law system and against the illegitimate
Rulers and criminal unlawful governing

ministers and agents, the last stand of the States Power lies with the police officers and military, if they no longer constistute the power of the state, as the states abled armed bodies of men and women, that are enforcing illegitimate unlawful acts and crimes upon the communities citizens the people, then the state collapses.

25

UNDER COMMON LAW HOW CITIZENS ARE TO CONDUCT A CITIZENS ARREST

In Common Law and in Civil Law it is known that it is essential and actual fundamental requisite and the absolute right of citizens, the people to apprehend and constrain and detain a criminal or a suspected criminal. The people can carry out citizen arrests also for endangering another citizen or the community citizens as a whole for causing harassment, injury, harm, rape, murder. Under Common Law the people are to unit in a goup form a posse as every adult citizen has the authority by obligation to immediately stop any acitivity of misconduct or evilness in the community and to apprehend any suspects for the safety of other citizens and the community. The relevance and gravity of the consequences of citizen arrests this gives responsibility to the citizens and actually empowers the people to protect and police there own communities and the Common Laws, this allows truefull real factual democracy to in manifested and realized.

Citizens arrest Protocal is –

There must be reasonable suspicion that the suspected person is a danger to a community citizen a risk to others, there can be no prejudice, it must be based on probable cause, you need to either recognize the suspected criminal or culprit, or have witnessed the crime.

The citizen preforming the citizens arrest must say who they are by name and that they are exercising the and enforcing the Right of the Necessity to Defend, and placing them under citizens arrest as you are obligated to by Common Law for the said crime or suspected offence, and also obligated to the community.

The arresting citizen will then take the suspect to the Sheriff-officer of the Common Law Court or to a Peace officer of the Common Law Court who are authorized, and hand over the suspect to be detained.

The amount of coerce force used in the arrest must be reasonable and a proportionate reaction to the suspects actions and behaviour, they are if its proved they posed a threat to others or commited a crime, to be detained ready for trial in the Common Law Court. The arresting citizen must give a sworn statement in Common Law Court concerning there actions of the arrest and testify to the facts of the case.

26

ESTABLISHED COMMON LAW BRINGS A DIRECT RELATIONSHIP TO THE PEOPLE TO THE COMMUNITIES

Humanity and humanites communities will have to start to perceive and act in the alternative fashion and from the perspective that no one has the authority or right over others, to dominate or control over or cause harm or distress to others and certainly not to rule over any one, as we truly are Highly Advanced Spiritual Eternal Light Beings of ultra violet energetic divine consciousness, manifested into human biological avatar bodies, and therefore SOVEREIGNTY of ourselves. There comes a time when the people the citizens of all communities will take direct action at all levels of society, the most persecuted normally unite and rise first, established Common Law Courts destabilize and in time collapse the illegitimate corrupt unlawful established criminal monarchy, institutions the church and state, and disempower the fallen angel descendants bloodlines and the power will be reinstated to the people, to be there own justices and police with mutual respect for one another governing there own affairs, united as one cohesive community, united as one collective of communities across a whole land, a whole nation, a whole collective of nations and the collective of earths tribal peoples and there communities.

This is a spiritual battle a spiritual war on our planet in the present for humanities freedom from dark species and entity forces, humanity must rise now, now is the time, ascension for humanity is coming in the years ahead so we must unite to prepare to raise our human avatars frequencies to evolve back to our true nature of an eternal race fully embodied as human beings, completely connected the the universe, the creation the hyper-dimensinal matrix of the whole brahaman.

It is a shift in thought processes it is a shift in consciousness individually then collectively for it is Universal Law so therefore Natural Law and its basic fundamental foundation is this Law will not cause harm to anyone, and this Law is for the good of all, this keeps equaliberium in the natural universe of life among all beings. As humanity is in clear apparent impending imminent and immediate danger the dark forces of evil there spiritual war now surfaced into the publics arena and encroaching on the liberties of humanities societies, communities that are intentionally killing murdering citizens and intentionally murdering there children, destroying the planet with no conscience of the Genocide they commit on humanity as a race and species, there intention is as clear as the sky when the sun rises, humanity all communities must take control and install Common Law Courts in the communities and govern by

Common Law, and daily life will change fundamentally dramatically for the better of all in the community, for all in world wide communities, and to make this a smoother transition in society the fallen angel royal descendants wealth and there institutions and corporations wealth should be distributed to all nations to rebuild there countries and there citizens can return home and rebuild and create new community for the benefit of all citizens worldwide globally.

This spiritual war on humanity has span many genorations already and with our awakened reality, our truth that we are not the mind or body of the human avatar, but we are eternal highly advanced spiritual light beings of divine ultra violet energetic consciousness, emanating from and the essence of the whole creations collective consciousness, and that under Universal Law which is Natural Law we understand reason and being just, and that now its time for all world citizens to unite in all communities and take first responsibility to govern themselves, by setting up Common Law Courts and the established enforcement of this Common Law Courts summons and served warrants.

This will allow humanity as a whole to win this spiritual war for it is the duty of all the elders on this planet that are above forty years old and the younger generations to stop this genocide of our human species, by darkness of evil entities that wish humanity to expire and decease, united we shall rise beyond then become illuminated fullfilling our cosmic destiny.

27

THE BIGGEST SECRET OF RULERS ILLEGITIMATE UNLAWFUL POWER UNDER YOUR FICTIOUS ILLUSIONARY CHARACTER YOUR STRAWMAN

They the illegitimate rulers and governance have no true power, if you stand in yours, stand in the Sovereignty Right of an Eternal Spiritual Being, did you know you have a choice it is Optional to pay fines and taxes and loans and morgages, as morgages are actually paid in complete totality from the day you sign contract, so paid in its entirety, and it is also Optional attending illegitimate unlawful Statute Courts and Optional in registering businesses and vehicles it is non-compulsory and certainly nonobligatory so therefore not required, so Optional in a matter of Fact.

So as I explained in chapter one about your fictitious character that's attached to your illegitimate birth certificate that's called your strawman, and gets its illusionary power by titles in front of your first name Mr, Master, Miss, Mrs and family name and is in capital letters of grammer. So the illegitimate authorities claim your parents signed away and lost ownership of you their living breathing physical animated human biological avatar baby, that is inhabited by your true identity the essence and spirit of an eternal interdimensional spirit light being of ultra violet divine energetic consciousness, and that in this process your parents unaware allowed the false creation of your fictious character known as your strawman, vis trickery and deceit, well the actual truth be known that this illegitimate registrated contract is all an illusion and is unlawful therefore is Null and Void, this is the true reality of the unlawful birth certificate as there was NO INTENT to contract from your parents as there was no disclosure of details and its true purpose not declared by the local authorities to your parents.

Your parents were deceived and they were falsely understood to believe that the birth certificate belonged to you their child which is not true, because as explained it is not a genuine birth certificate it is actually the creation of an illusionary character called your strawman which is masquerading as you, but spelt in capitals and with a title in front of your first and family name, it is illegitimate and unlawful therefore does not stand, and is Null ans Void.

So therefore it is an unlawful illegitimate legal entity that was created to enslave you with out your parents and your knowledge, and created to criminally fool you into paying various illusionary imaginary liabilities and costs, which are attached to the fraudulent character of your fake strawman charcter that does not exist, is not animated and living, alive. This is one of the biggest scams on humanity at this time by corrupt illegitimate rulers and governance criminals in power.

A fictitious charcter is created by the illegitimate and unlawful state, in order to charge the imaginary costs of unlawful amounts of penalties and charges to the tricked and fooled real animated living alive person, them thinking and believing that this is the real them when it is not it is the fictitious charcter known as your strawman. These illegitimate and unlawful charges consist of council tax, inheritance tax, income tax, capital gains tax, value added tax, road tax, import tax, fuel levy, loan interest, bank charges and also anything else that any illegitimate and unlawful professionals have and can think of to create false unlawful charges, that you will not understand and will not notice, which you have never entered contract with or agreed to give, yield, bear or to pay off, because these said illegitimate taxes, fines, charges are unlawful and you are not obliged or obligated to submit or surrender or pay in anyway under any circumstances, because they were created and born from deceit and trickery thus making them Null and Void.

The illegitimate unlawful Corporation Statute Laws, the Law of Contracts that came from Maritime Law, known as Admiralty Law most commonly known as Law of the Sea, uses trickery and deceit by way of language, it is known as Legalese the secret language created to trick you into contract, this Legalese language uses the English language of words that have attached to them different secret meanings, with the sole intention and purpose of trying to stop you from believing that what they are saying to you has nothing to do with the normal meaning of the words used in the English language, this Corporate systems intention and absolute purpose is to steal your hard earned money, by way of robbery and trickery to cheat you out of your hard earned income, your money, your personal wealth.

The truth is that you will never be informed by these corporations and police statute law corporations or illegitimate unlawful courts of statute law corporations that they have indeed changed the English language to the Legalese language which is unlawful, criminal in nature, completely dishonest, shows no regard for what is Right and Honorable, it has no regard for the existing, already Universal standing of Universal Law that is Natural Law and is Common Law, Law of the Land that has Constitutional Law.

So worldwide citizens of humanity are being tricked, as you believe you are being spoken to and are replying by speaking and answering in the English language, when in actual matter of fact they are coercing you and pretending that you are entering and contracting to them, to then become a lower or inferior subordinate to them that they can manipulate and control.

This is type of trickery and deceit is Null and Void as all parties must be fully informed of all information, it must be openly disclosed and all of the terms and conditions of the contract must be shown and absolutely unreserved and accepted by agreement by both parties, as this is definitely a verbal contract between your self and them there must be transparency for any contract to be valid or it is Null and Void. This is how they trick you to represent a fictitious illusionary charcter known as your strawman that's connected to your illegitimate unlawful birth certificate.

Common Law which is Natural Law, Law of the Land on planets Universally, is for the benefit and security of all, in the communities, its very simple treat others as you wish to be treated, love thy neighbour or at least show them common courtesy and respect, to be truthful, honorable, genuine and sincere in your relations and transactions in the community, and allow a little give and take in certain situations with common sense and logic, and do not try to defraud, scam or short change fellow citizens, you are obligated not to destroy or damage or out right pinch, take, or thieve another citizens property, and the evident and apparent ones being do not hurt or cause harm, wound or injure another citizen and certainly do not kill or murder another citizen, this is basis Universal Law which is Natural Law and in turn is Common Law, Law of the Land. So a few basic Laws not to rob another, not to harm another, and be honorable in your relations and transactions, very simple. These few laws are the only constraints on you and if you decide you are not going to live by them, then best you leave the communities keep your distance from other citizens and live in a remote location, we all have a choice to live in harmony with others and nature to keep the equilibrium of nature, the balance of all life.

This is why the dark evil forces that try to enslave humanity and its unaware citizens because of the Satanic reversal of words vis trickery of language, but these illegitimate and unlawful fines, charges and taxes are not compulsory, it is a choice whether you decide to verbally agree and enter into contract with them, if you do so then you are agreeing you are a fictitious charcter, commonly know as your strawman, they will try to coerce, to stand for and symbolize your fictitious charcter, this would then leave you open to there said made up rules and laws and there said illegitimate unlawful charges, and exceptional expensive fines.

This is how the rulers get away with the control of humanity, so do not agree, do not Consent to being the fictitious character and you will not be bound to them the fallen angel descendants satanic cult, do not Consent to there illegitimate unlawful Statute Laws that are made up by rulers and there corrupt governance agents, that are intentionally designed to keep the people poor and restricted and suppressed and that enriches and gives power to the criminal illegitimate unlawful rulers and there minions.

So governments and police stations and fire serives etc. the arms of governance and so on are all corporations, and they want to make money and extract as much wealth as possible from the citizens, from the communities of the people. This agenda has the energy of lucifer, from evil darkness for domination of and over humanity and the planet Gaia our Mother Earth, Pachamama.

28

DO NOT CONSENT TO STATUTE LAW POLICE OFFICERS

DO NOT CONSENT to a Statute Law enforcing police officer because Service Corporation do not make or write Law! You need to understand this as you can stand in your Sovereignty Power when you know the Truth of Law, as when unlawful police officers are stopping your natural right of movement and are confrontational to you, in your personal space, or even on private property or in public spaces, they are acting on behalf of a Service Corporation that is illegitimately unlawfully imposing Coporation Satute Law, that you are not governed under, as you are a Sovereignty of your own Natural Right, the unlawful police officers are believing in the illegitimate Statute Law because it Corruptly was handed down from the government and given by the illegitimate legislator, which is a Service Corporation, this is therefore illegitimate unlawful and it is absolutely NOT LAW, it is Policy, this means the confronting unlawful Statute Law police enforcing officers are commiting a crime and while wearing a police uniform, this is up to twenty years in prison and up to a 10,000 pound fine. When confronting police officers act in this unlawful manner, thay have no rights to trespass upon you against you, they have no right to unlawfully charge you with illegitimate Statute Laws, policies, statues, offences and citations as they are unlawful, therefore the police officers are acting wrong unjust and criminally commiting a crime and in a police uniform, which is up to twenty years in prison and up to a 10,000 pound fine. If charged falsely unlawfully by Statute Law Police officers you can file your own documentation your self or by serving a Notary, this is then noted in the Statute Law system and have to recognize this is the fact of the matter in hand, a Notary is a legal form, you are not then pulled into the Statute Law legal system, a Notary is putting a stamp and seal on something usually a document, verifying that the document is true that is being brought before them, the seal represents that the person declaring it is being truthfull and lawful, if not that police officer is liable.

29

THE TRUE REALITY OF LIFE

To travel in time and space is to understand Offset spacial divergence, most average citizens of humanity are not Capable of comprehending or accepting the discoveries of other past, present, and future timelines at this present time in the now, the origin of the universe is known, the Nature of so called life it is known, the meaning of life is to understand and comprehend the Nature of life, the difference is the meaning that is something ascribed, but Nature is the objective reality of life, knowing and understanding how the universe is created, not by a God as this is the old paradigm of thinking as we evolve past the need of superstition and the need for the myths of a Gods, for we still believe that we die but we don't Death is a human construct it does not exist, we have experience, you have experienced and manifested as every possible instance and construct of so called life, you have already been, so manifested as every species in this universe over the last thirteen point six eight billion years and now you are manifested as human in the present of now timeline, every human on earth and every race in this universe we all have experienced all manifested races-species in this said universe, we are all the same instances of the same life, only separated by what humans call Death, this is the essence of Nature the essence of Life.

There are an infinite number of universes each having different physical properties, virtually all do not support life, such as humanity at this time perceives and knows in there understanding of the universe, we exist in a universe that does support so called life, it is Dogma that is destroying humanity at this time political and religious dogma manmade constructs for control of the masses of humanity, this is the root of all main conflicts of humanity of our species, this is because

of nations and states that are suppressing
humanity at this time through the fear of
illusionary dogma, their leaders are
Satanists with there own negative
agendas.

Then when we see past the illusions and
dogma we come to understand, and so
can perceive with clarity, and we can then
come from morality and percieve the
morality of life and its basis which is
simply compassion and evidence.

30

UNDERSTANDING THE SUFFERING
OF LIFE

One must understand that all suffering is
our own doing and are lessons to learn
from, we manifest individually all the
suffering, pain, anguish by our monkey
mind of uncontrolled and checked
thoughts and emotions, the God
conscious level of understanding is that
this suffering is also governed by Karmic
Law from our past manifested lifes, and
with the returned energy from the
Universal Law of Attraction, from the ills
and woes of our past ill intentions and
actions, that we cause and inflict on
others shall be returned upon us to
experience in full, by the Law of
Attraction.
So be mindful of your thoughts and
actions have gratitude, be kind, love thy
neighbour, for we are all here to learn to

be loving, to come from good intention, to be caring in nature and connected to the heart, coming from the heart in all we manifest into creation, this allows spirit to come fourth and shine expelling the divine essence of the oneness eternal God consciousness, expressing in the image of the creator.

31

THE BRITISH QUEEN & HER OATH & CONTRACT TO THE PEOPLE MAGNA CARTA COMMON LAW

The Queen under her Oath, Elizabeth the second has not held her Oath and Contract with the native United Kingdom citizens to protect citizens and security of borders, she has failed the people and under Common Law and Magna Carta, she and her government have fell Null and Void in the contract to the people, allowing enemy invaders to enter the United Kingdom lands, and foreign Saudi government agents to infiltrate politics, infiltrate government state levels and below in city and town levels of governance.

It is clear in Common Law she is to uphold security for all native United Kingdom citizens and we believe in

Common Wealth Countries and lands of those citizens.

The Queen Elizabeth the second and her government have broken the Laws of the Land and therefore she is Null and Void of the peoples contract in Common Law. She has broken the Ten Commandments, broken the Golden Rule, she and her government have broken Common Law Charter of Liberties which makes the monarch subject to Law and the 1627 Petition Right, which grants the Right to critise the government with out of fear of arrest, as well as Magna Carta Common Law and Declaration of Right, the Common Law defends property Rights and Rights of Self Defence, which she and her government have broken, against the people, they have seized housing property and other property of the people in a an illegitimate unlawful and fraudulent way. They have also broken Common Law in the Right to self defence, by trying to stop people filming and recording, a record in court proceedings, and illegitimately unlawfully seizing and imprisoning and stripping Rights and possessions of the people and have illegitimately unlawfully so criminally proceeded with force and unlawful judgement of the people, as trials and charge are happening in the United Kingdom courts with out jury of equals.

The Queen and her government have denied and delayed the Right to Justice, she and her government has broken Common Law of the Land. Magna Carta affirmed the Right of the people to such things as trials by jury, and protection from excessive fines.
Remember native United Kingdom citizens she swore an Oath to uphold these Common Laws and millions and millions all over the world saw her do this, in the video of her coronation in 1953 june 2nd and has not held that Oath. Magna Carta in Statute Law, parliament can repeal or amend any act of parliament (statue), but parliament was not party to

the original Common Law Contract, and cannot therefore, be Amended, Modified, or Repealed, it is Lawfully and thus its Original Provisions remain Intact.

The Queen Elizabeth second and her government have breeched contract with the people under Common Law, so allegiance can be with drawn if the monarch is in breech of contract with the people. So taxes now are excessive the fines on the people criminal and extortionate on the people, she is one of the head families of the Goldsmith Davidic Royal Zionist Jewish Israelite bloodlines above her is the Rothschild bloodline they are all also known as the kahazarian and Ashkenazi crime families, also the House of Saud Royal bloodlines.

So we the people demand under Common Law Magna Carta and to get performed the Solemn Fuedal ceremony of Diffidatio, or renunciation of their fealty and homage, a formality indispensable before vassals could, without infamy, wage war upon their feudal overlord (the Queen and her government).

Absolved of our allegiance the people all 64 million approximated citizens shall should then march to London to the palace and west minister houses of parliament, what this demonstrates is having taken an Oath of allegiance which one might assume is for life, is not, and so allegiance can be with drawn if the monarch is in breach of their contract with the people, and they are the Queen and the government are in breech of the **Magna Carta Contract.** They the Queen Elizabeth the second and her government are also under Common Law in breach, of from the 15th of June 1215 of ARTICALS with additional FURMA SECURITATIS or executive clause, vesting in twenty-five number FULL AUTHORITY to CONSTRAIN Queen Elizabeth the second and her government by FORCE TO OBSERVE ITS PROVISIONS.

The PEOPLE have the RIGHT TO
REBEL – that have FULL AUTHORITY
TO CONSTRAIN.. by FORCE is one of
the key features of The MAGNA
CARTA COMMON LAW CONTRACT.

Our right to rebel should the Queen and

her government of the day be operating

outside it (39,s lawful authority. Article

61, basically saying that since we have

granted all these things to God, (and me

and you are God) for the better ordering

of our Kingdom, and to allay discord with

the Queen her government and the

people and we give and grant security to

the Queen and her government. Article 61

continues (if we the people our chief

justice, our government officals, or any of

our government servants offend in any

respect against a man or transgress any
articals of the peace or of this security,
and the offence is made known to four of
the said barons, they shall come to us, or
in our absence from the kingdom to the
chief justice – to declare it and claim
immediate redress by seizing our castles,
lands, possessions, or anything else save
only our own person and those of the
Queen and our children, until they have
secured such redress, they may then
resume their normal abedience to us (the
people). The phrase (until they have
secured such redress as they have
determined upon) gives AUTHORITY for
the constitutional convention. There have
been 3 such conventions in the last 800

years, in other words, its our duty to step in and require the monarch to uphold their contract with the people.

Sovereignty lies with the people and the monarch is bound by that Oath to hold an - out of control government to account.

The people, native United Kingdom citizens from England Scottland Wales Ireland and all the Isles in between hold you the monarch, you the Queen Elizabeth the second and all your government, in breech of Common Law and Magna Carta for crimes against the people on security of the native United Kingdoms lands, allowing different enemies political, militant, radical, totalitarian regime in our lands, with illegitimate unlawful open boarders with no security by intention, the people also charge you with allowing this House of Saud Royal bloodlines foreign government to take power in government and governance of our lands, citys, towns, councils. We the people also charge you with allowing foreign influence in financial monitaries to influence and corrupt our government and society, the people also charge the Queen for allowing the organised militant muslim pedophile enemy gangs to pedoplie and rape over one and half million native United Kingdom citizens children and covering it up, shutting down media and the criminal and illegal imprisonment of citizens and media, who have reported and kept record of truth, under the legal Common Law, we the people charge you for allowing 23 known pedophiles in the labour party in 2017-2018 running government today and in recent past from 1970-2020 up to today, other government officals and servants that are pedophiles, the people charge you with illegitimately unlawfully, so criminally illegally corrupting government and by the use of blackmail, the people charge you Queen Elizabeth the second and your government officials with making illegitimate unlawful, so criminal illegal acts of parliament, regulations, rules, polices and sub laws that are unlawful criminal and do not stand up to Common Law which is Law of this United Kingdom land – since 871-899 AD established by (Alfred the great) and up dated in 1297 the model parliament comfirmed Magna Carta in Statute Law.

The people charge you Queen Elizabeth with the illegal criminal use of mind control technologies and programming, to ditort the truth and perception of reality and to distort the truth and perception of the people and to damage the genetics the RNA and DNA of our human biological avatars, our bodies, damaging health, including toxifing of heavy metals, calcium, and fluoride in the peoples drinking water and chemicals and agents poisonous in the peoples foods. We charge you with the intent of changing the peoples RNA and DNA by pharmaceutical drugs and biological weapon vaccines and by genetically modified grains, wheats, foods, we also charge you with allowing the use of smart meters, 3G 4G 5G microwave warfare weapons technologies on the people.

The people charge you Queen Elizabeth the second and all your family bloodlines and extended bloodlines with the sickest of crimes the crime of (CHILD SACRIFICE) the sin of all sins (from the perspective of the immortal and mortal consciousness) and the crime of (PEDOPHILIA), the people know of the Royal pedophile run pedophile rings and are charged with the murders of thousands of children.

The people charge you Queen Elizabeth and all members of the Royal Fallen Angels bloodlines with the crimes of ADRENOCHROME USE the royal cult practice of drinking childrens blood after they have been tortured and raped there is more adrenaline in the blood, this is the Royal Elites drug human childrens blood, you are therefore charged with the above crimes.

So Queen Elizabeth the second and your family bloodlines and extended bloodlines and your government are charged with War Crimes of Illegal wars for the secret reason that they are blood sacrifice in our faces, to gain and extract humanities loosh energy.

The People are awake and they are also aware that they are Eternal Immortal Interdimensional Light Beings of Divine Conscious Energy from the eternal realms outside time and space from the Kingdom of Light, the kingdom of Heaven, we are the Second Coming, we have been waiting for.

Hundreds and thousands of us are now opening portholes outside of linear time, outside of this university, this universe of light, to access the Immortal realm the Kingdom of Light and allowing humans that have stopped the cycles of life and death and opened their light bodies to become eternal light beings, Christ and Buddha beings of light, to come into this dimension to assist in healing and transformation, metamorphosing to our rainbow light bodies and assist in other light works and in transendance and in the evolving to HomoLuminous.

As the people are ultra violet light energy consciousness a single cell vibrating at frequency creating sacred geometry of the dodecahedron, which has 20 amino acids on its corners and inside the dodecahedron is a tetrahedron spinning and inside that a Torus field spinning in 120 different patterns to create 120 different proteins. Also a tower block of crystal dodecahedrons by universal design attracts DNA, by design to start forming biological life.

So we the people are awake on many levels mentally, emotionally, consciously, some of us are travelling in our solar systems, galaxies, universe, and other dimensions, the citizens are remote viewing, meditating leaving their bodies consciously and some people are meeting with extraterrestials, interdimensional beings, spirit beings and light beings physically and leaving our bodies in energetic form and communicating in dreams. So expect more and more native united citizens and world citizens to wake up to there second coming and their eternal duty, there mission on behalf of the Kingdom of Light and in service to The Oneness to the Creation which is pro life and under universal law.

To stop Queen Elizabeth the second and all of her kin, family Royal bloodlines and extended Royal bloodlines the House of Saud and to stop her government, her corrupt ministers and servants, to stop your corrupt illegitimate unlawful, criminal illegal rule under Law of the Land, Common Law and Magna Carta Law. The world citizens, the people of the United Kingdom, from the Kingdom of Light outside linear time the Immortal Realm, we serve you with Notice and Writs of Common Law and Criminal law, we serve you Queen Elizabeth the second and your government your bloodlines, your Royal Goldsmith Davidic Jewish bloodlines the Kahazarian and Ashkenazi crime families, the House of Saud with TREASON, with corruption and human Rights Violations and Crimes against Humanity, we charge you with Genocide on the native United Kingdom citizens and on the world wide citizens that of humanity.

You Queen Elizabeth and all your bloodlines and your government, officals and servant, you are Responsible to Fulfill your Sworn Duties and uphold the Contract to the native people of the United Kingdom and to the Eternal Kingdom of Light in the Immortal Realm holds you all accountable for your sins of crimes to humanity who originate on earth. You will still pay in karmatic cycles adding up to 26 thousand years a cycle and some up to 3 cycles, so adding up to 78 thousand years of life times of suffering for what you did to souls here on earth, and so the the Law of Attraction karma shall be returned to you, life time after life time of suffering.

You the bloodlines of the Fallen Angels Descendants are here by Served by The People, the native citizens of the United Kingdom, and served by the world wide earth citizens from every nation, and you are here by Served by us from the Eternal Immortal Dimensional Realm from outside time and space, we Eternal Light Beings of God Consciousness Spirit manifest with all our intention with our Oneness of Consciousness, that your 26 to 78 thousand years of life times of suffering of karmic dept to be payed in full with immediate effect and so it shall be humbly so.

Also a large population millions and millions of earths population know that the Royal bloodlines the British European and House of Saud have been infiltrated and corrupted by Entities of the JINN also known as the Archons, and the Annunaki an exraterrestrial negative race, energetic 4th dimensional beings in known physical form, manifesting in 3Dimensional reality in the fallen angel bloodlines because of resonance of their DNA type and frequency.

Planet Gaia Mother Earth also known as Pachamama was long ago invaded by extraterrestrial forces, and the human race has been living with this infestation, of negative races and energetic Demons, the Archons the Jinn and the Fallen Angel Draconian Royal Goldsmith Davidic Zionist Jewish Israelite bloodlines are compromised at this level, working with the Draco beings of negative agendas. They will be held accountable under Universal Law, maybe also in galactic court in our quadrant of this galaxies court, charged for genocide to humanity on earth, as it has been said that the five main familes responsible for this genocide may be summons to the galactic court of our quadrant or the proceedings held on planet Gaia Mother Earth and they will be charged and sentenced, under Universal Law and Galactic Law, in the not to distant future for over six thousand years of child sacrifice, sins of all sins and all their other crimes of humanity.

The People native United Kingdom citizens and citizens of the world see past the Dogma of Political and Religions and see through the bloodlines farse, of pure theatre, made up, fiction, under the name of God their to rule, there is no one God, we are all God and all reality around us conscious energy, is God vibrating at resonance and different frequencies to create different sacred geometry the building blocks of matter, of life, with light energy, Eternal Immortal Light Beings we be transcending in all dimensions of reality and in the Immortal Realms outside linear time and space, in the now all at once.

The people of earth charge you Queen Elizabeth the second and all your bloodlines and your government and its ministers and servants, we charge you for crimes againat humanity in the name of the Creator, the Brahman, the Whole, the Oneness of all that be.

Conclusion – there are many unwritten customs which are considered to be ancient traditions that have always belonged to the people, one obvious example is the Right to Free Speech, for which, unlike the USA constitution , there is no written provision within the British Constitution, so while we have shown in previous pages that our Rights and Liberties are clearly stated in Written Contracts, it is also true that many of our Rights, whilst not in Written Form, are Equally Valid.

Today the British Constitution is in grave danger, moves are a foot to replace the Bill of Rights and the Act of Settlement. These are to be replaced by an illegitimate unlawful, so illegal new Bill of Rights and a European Constitution, Britian - 39,s Constitutional Documents are Timeless, and were constructed by The People.

The new illegitimate unlawful, criminal illegal constitutional documents will be written by corrupt politians, which is illegal, a criminal act. The politians are corrupt and need to be imprisoned for illegally making illegal laws that do not stand up to the Original Laws of the Land Common Law and Magna Carta Law. Parliament has grabbed executive power from the crown, the house of lords has become a body which blindly follows the party whip. And today, our monarch (is meant to) simply complies with the wishes of the Prime Minister, with no thought or consideration to our Sovereignty or the Constitution, nor it seems, to the Solemn Oath she the Queen took at her coronation.

(Executive power) will corrupt the legislatures as necessarily as rust corrupts iron metal, and when the legislature is corrupted, the people are undone.

It is up to the people to resolve the corrupt monarch and her government, charge her the Queen Elizabeth the second and her entire bloodlines and extended bloodlines and her government and its officals for the crimes against the people of the United Kingdom and the world citizens, crimes against humanity and when charged in court, removed from the court if found guilty, as she will be, of Treason, to be sentenced, just as other people have, past monarchs Charles the first put to death an was executed, we the people also disposed of 5 other monarchs Etherlred, Richard the second, Henry VI the six, James the second and Edward the 8th.

Look at the Queens Prime minister Boris Johnson he his pushing there agendas on the United Kingdom and world citizens by speaking at the united nations pushing for military grade warfare microwave frequency weapons to be used on the public for mind control and distortion of the genetic geometric structure of your biological cells, to cause mutations of your bodies and Boris Johnson is also pushing the Elite Satanic cults agenda of biological weapon virus non-vaccines that will alter your RNA and DNA, so you can then be patented as a product slave as your DNA will not be of the original strain of genetics. Boris Johnson is an enemy of the worlds children and humanity, he is being a representative of the Royal Davidic Zionist Jewish Demonic Satanic bloodlines cult one of its leader the Queen Elizabeth the second.

May you the native united citizens and world citizens be blessed in your battle of good against evil on behalf of the immortal realm the Kingdom of Light, have love in your hearts, work on this mission in peace and you will prevail and ascend to the eternal Kingdom of Light, but also remember it takes good souls of men and women to stand against evil men and women and to fight against there maya of their minds and their demons, and rise you shall like the pheniox and unit as one.

The fallen angel descendants cult only

has an illusion of power as it expresses its power to the people on a repetitive daily continuum via media, but its all an illusion, they are the few less than 1% but we are the 99% we THE PEOPLE truly have the POWER, if only we would Unite as ONE.

32

TWELVE UNIVERSAL LAWS

Law of Divine Oneness

The number one law that is the absolute foundational law of the universe is the Law of Divine Oneness, which illuminates the absolute interconnectedness of all things, it reveals that beyond our senses, every action and thought and reactional event is connected to everything else connected to all in existence. So we must come from the heart chakra from the intentioned energy of love in our creating and manifesting life in the physical dimensions, realms and learn to be compassionate with each other, for we are all created from the oneness and all are created from divine source energy of ultra violet divine energetic consciousness, so with focus of our attention and stillness comes clarity keeping this in mind, we are all one in the oneness of creation, the whole, the brahman.

Law of Perpetual Transmutation of Energy

This law reveals that on an energetic level, everything in the universe is constantly evolving, osilating and fluctuating in waves in all of creation, every manifested action is preceded by an energetic thought, with thoughts themselves having the divine creative power to eventually manifest in our physical realities.

Law of Vibration

We see that at the microscopic level that all things are in constant motion, vibrating at specifically organized frequencies, this applies to all matter and to ones own personal frequency as well, this law tells us that our individual vibrational frequency actually informs our manifesting living experience. You can change and raise your frequency by many practices by doing, meditation, energy arts and practices and spiritual practices and shamanic ceremonies and diet is key to raising your vibration.

Law of Correspondence

This law reveals that patterns repeat throughout the cosmos the universe, so we are personally responsible for individually creating our reality that is a mirror of focus of what is occuring internally within us in the present moment of now. So the reflection you see inwards shall be reflected into your outward manifested reality.

Law of Attraction

The law of attraction is the key law for manifesting, it reveals that like attracts like and you will receive what you focus your attention on, so you have to really *believe* what you want to create and experience and believe it is possible to achieve and obtain, and perceive you already are experiencing this, you actually have to feel what you are seeking then it shall manifest, this has a likeness to the law of vibration, as it is essential to learn to vibrate at higher levels that attracts what you are wishing to manifest into creation.

Law of Cause and Effect

Relatively is self explanatory this law illuminates the direct relation between actions and the reactions of events, we often cannot see the effects immediately but they will always come back around and be returned upon us, to us directly. What you think, speak, act is put out there in creation and may not come back to you in that present moment but that vibration frequencies of energy you expelled out there into the creational magnet fields of manifestation, this has a ripple effect, and will be mirrored back to you.

Law of Rhythm

Cycles are a contant natural part of the universes physically, as you can perceive about the seasons on our planet Gaia our Mother Earth, Pachamama, and of course in our own lives we know that integration is just as important as personal growth, start to be mindful of your inner rhythms and work with them instead of fighting them.

Law of Inspired Action

Similarly related to the law of attraction is the law of inspired action which is all about taking those actions on your intended truths, putting momentum to present actionable steps to draw in what we wish into our lives, when attention is focused inspiration comes from within.

THE LAW OF COMPENSATION

The law of compensation relates similarly to the law of attraction also to the law of correspondence, as ancient texts reveal (You reap what you sow) is the absolute truth and lesson to remeber, with this law revealing your efforts will always come back to you positively, when you are wishing to manifest something you always have to contribute in some way toward your goal.

Law of Relativity

This law explains that we are always inclined to compare things in our world, but in reality, everything is neutral, so indifferent and fair minded, so relativism the belief that all different things are true and right that exists in all things, so this means it comes down to our perspective and perception, of that of the eye of the beholder.

Law of Polarity

This law reveals that everything in the creation of life has an opposite a negative or positive also perceived as good or evil, and also the vibration of love or fear, light and dark, so hot and cold, fusion.

Law of Gender

The law of gender has to do with the feminine and the masculine energies that exists in all things in the creation, the whole, the brahaman, by achieving your own internal inner balance between masculine and feminine energies will help you be true to your eternal nature.

33

CLOSING STATEMENTS

OUR PLANET GAIA OUR MOTHER EARTH, PACHAMAMA meaning –

GODDESS known as EARTH TIME MOTHER a GODDESS of Fertility, of LIFE.

PACHAMAMA is the GODDESS of CREATIVE POWER to sustain all LIFE on her BEING, on her planetary body, that is our WORLD, respect her we must, we must restore her health with that of ours as we are her guardians her caretaker that lost their way, return back to nature connect and spirit you shall see, the illusions falling away, then we can unite and care and love our mother Pachamama for symbiotic we truly be.

EVERY CHILD & MAN & WOMAN
ARE BORN FREE.

BUT YET EVERYWHERE ON THE
PLANET GAIA, MOTHER EARTH,
PACHAMAMA, THEY ARE
SUPPRESSED.

THIS OPPRESSION & VIOLENCE IS
ON A CONTINUUM IN ALL ASPECTS
OF OUR LIFES, EFFECTING OUR
PHYSICAL, MENTAL, EMOTIONAL,
MULTIDIMENSIONAL WAY OF
BEING.

HUMANITY UNITED CAN CHANGE
THIS, UNITED, UNIFED &
MANIFEST & TAKE APPROPRIATE
ACTIONS & FREEDOM FROM
TYRANNY, TO STOP HUMANITIES
GENOCIDE.

FOR IF GOOD SOULS FROM THE
KINGDOM OF LIGHT OUTSIDE TIME

& SPACE MANIFEST HERE ON
EARTH & DO NOTHING SATANIC
DEMONIC EVIL WILL PREVAIL.

IT HAS BEEN SAID –

AT THIS TIME IN THE PEOPLES
HEARTS IN THE PRESENT –

THE PEOPLE ARE SPEAKING RIGHT
NOW IN THE MOMENT –

AND STANDING IN THEIR POWER
AND SAYING TO THE CORRUPTED
IN GOVERNMENT AND CORRUPT
CORPORATE STATUTE LAW
CRIMINAL ENFORCEMENT
OFFICERS –

DON'T TRY TO RUIN OUR LIVES
WITH LIES – WHEN YOUR LIFE CAN
BE RUINED BY THE TRUTH – THE
TRUTH OF YOUR CORRUPTION &
UNLAWFUL CRIMES.

WHEN WILL DOUBT FREE THE
PEOPLE - OH GOD OF MERCY,
WHEN.

THE PEOPLE OR THE PEOPLE BY

THE PEOPLE NOT CROWNS AND

THRONES BUT MEN AND WOMEN

ORDAIN TO AUTHORIZE THE

GOVERNMENT AND ITS POWERS

AND ITS SERVANTS BY THE

PEOPLE IN SERVICE TO THE

PEOPLE UNDER CONSTITUTIONAL

LAW WHICH IS NATURAL LAW SO

LAW OF THE LAND WHICH IS

UNIVERSAL LAW.

34

About This Author

I WAS BORN IN A THUNDER BURST OF COSMIC DUST IN THE ONENESS OF ALL THAT BE, MANIFESTING IN THE ILLUSIONARY UNIVERSITY OF LIGHT IN ALL ITS DENSITIES AND VIBRATORY FORMS, FOR I THE ETERNAL SINGULAR CELL OF THE WHOLE COSMIC CONSCIOUSNESS COLLECTIVE, BEING CONNECTED TO ALL THAT BE IN THE CREATION, THE BRAHMAN, THE WHOLE, FOR WE ARE ALL ONE in the oneness of all that be in the sea of cosmic light, a swirling of energy, electromagnetism, the weak and strong nuclear forces and gravity, DIVINE ETERNAL IMMORTAL INTER- DIMENSIONAL ANGELIC LIGHT BEINGS OF ULTRA VIOLET ENERGETIC CONSCIOUSNESS, CREATING AN AVATAR A BIOLOGICAL HUMAN

FORM BODY FOR EXPERIENCE, TO PAY KARMA, AND MANIFESTING IN FROM THE ETERNAL TO RAISE HUMANITIES COLLECTIVE CONSCIOUSNESS, FOR SPIRIT I BE FOR ENERGY I SEE, ALL AROUND ME MULTI-DIMENSIONALLY THIS IS JUST HOW IT BE YOU SEE, FREQUENCY VIBRATING LIGHT IN WAVE AND POWDERED FORM TO, OPENING PORTHOLES OUTSIDE TIME AND SPACE FROM WHERE WE COME, HOME IT BE IN THE ETERNAL REALM OF THE KINGDOM OF LIGHT, allowing humans that have ascended opened their eternal light bodies and stopped the cycles of life and death, to evolve from HomoSapien, to HomoLuminous, we call upon illuminated beings, on buddha beings, and our ancestors at this time for transformation to evolve to metamorphosis in the rainbow angelic light beings we be in our true nature, we open our light bodies via our DNA within are the schematics of the blue print of your light body and access it we will and quantum leap ten thousand years into our becoming, allowing us to be fully embodied on this 4th/5th dimensional earth planet and at the same time we can travel the stars at instant will teleporting to and fro and accessing the eternal kingdom of light realms, blessed I be for magic I see all around me in powdered light illusionary form divine spirit it be gravity, I see eternal transcendental oneness of all that be in creation, do you see blessings namaste lovelifelee.

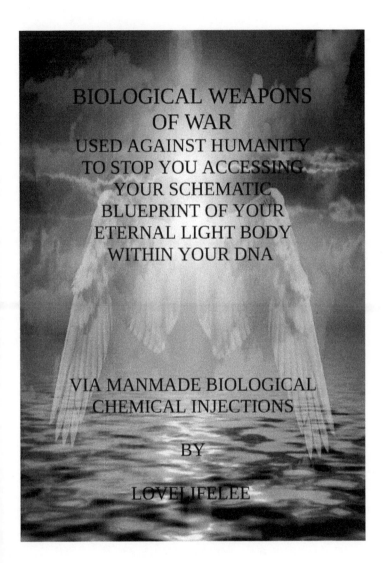

BIOLOGICAL WEAPONS
OF WAR
USED AGAINST HUMANITY
TO STOP YOU ACCESSING
YOUR SCHEMATIC
BLUEPRINT OF YOUR
ETERNAL LIGHT BODY
WITHIN YOUR DNA

VIA MANMADE BIOLOGICAL
CHEMICAL INJECTIONS

BY

LOVELIFELEE

FRONT COVER

This short book explains the truth behind the psychological warfare conducted on the public & biological weapon vaccines, the intention behind them from the fallen angels cult to not only to cull a large portion of humanity in their eugenics program, but from the highest levels of understanding, from the spiritual god conscious perspective, from the awakened human being to that of their eternal immortality, on the understanding that the vaccines will stop you accessing your light body, via a schematic blueprint in your DNA, also this book explains our cells and their function and relationship to poisons.
This book also has an introduction to the DNA blue print of instructions to grow a light body.

BACK COVER

The Illusionist
Rona The Maya of
Demons The ROYAL
Fallen Angel
Bloodlines

& Their Psychological
& Physical War on Humanity
& Information of your light body

BY
LOVELIFELEE

FRONT COVER

MER - KA - BA

(Human)   (Light)   (Body)

Is.This is an explosive, revealing book of ancient knowledge of the blueprint & schematics in your DNA to grow your eternal light body to ascend transcend in the higher dimensional matrix & recover ancient knowledge of the fallen angels, according to the two royal bavaric zionist orders of satanic cult blood sacrific their agendas including Roman military warfare grade microwave weapons, biological weapon vaccines that will rewrite the code of your DNA, then the elite can patent you. n shaus your eternal consciousness imprisoned, held Captive & Archon & Jinn demonic spirit attachments the fallen angels

BACK COVER

216

The Illusion of Rona The Maya of
Demons The Royal Fallen Angel
Bloodlines

The Illusion of Rona The Maya of
Demons The Royal Fallen Angel
Bloodlines, is a book written in the
now 2020 as times are changing by
force on society by criminal corrupt
mentally ill evil people, that are in
secret society cults, in a war part
psychological on the human race,
they come from ancient fallen angel
bloodlines and there blackmailed
puppet ministers in government and
corporations that are lost in the minds
of maya for greed power and control
of the human race, this book
discusses the illusion of reality
created by these bloodlines and there
agendas and there strategies forced
on the masses still programmed from
birth and then indoctrinated and brain
washed into an illusion of reality and
there weapons of choice used on
society, like mind control, biological

weapons as vaccines and illusion of false viruses and military grade microwave weapon systems, the poisoning of water, food, and the illusion of global warming, some of there history up to times in 2020 and there evil goals and the truth of our DNA makeup our bodies, consciousness and our light bodies and ascension.

This is an explosive and riveting compelling revealing book of ancient knowledge of the blueprint and schematics in your DNA to grow your eternal light body and this book reveals ancient knowledge of the fallen angels bloodlines the house of Saudi royals and the British German European royals of the Davidic Zionist Jewish orders from their Demonic Satanic Death Cult of Blood Sacrifice, their agendas including the Rona virus and use of military grade microwave frequency weapons and man made biological weapon virus vaccines and there psychological, physical and spiritual war on humanity of tyranny, for dominate complete control of society and the whole human race civilization. There intent to depopulate to a few hundred million and to imprison eternal souls manifesting here on earth by way of manipulating our DNA, so the human race cannot access higher levels of consciousness or the zero point energy field or the hyper-dimensional matrix of the creation, creating a slave race owned by corporations, trapped then in an eternal cycle of enslavement. An eye opener for many civilians especially if still under programming and indoctrination, of mind control.

Most importantly information on your DNA and your avatar your body about the blueprint and schematics to grow your light body and stop the cycles of life and death and ascend, and therefore not being trapped in this dimension of reality by Demons the

Archons the Jinn and the royal bloodlines they manifest into the Davidic Jewish orders of the satanic cult, also known as the illuminati, cabal and elite globalists.

These bloodlines are also known as the Kahazarian and Ashkenazi crime families that rule with brutal terror and genocide and perpetual murder assassinations to cover up these crimes on humanity.

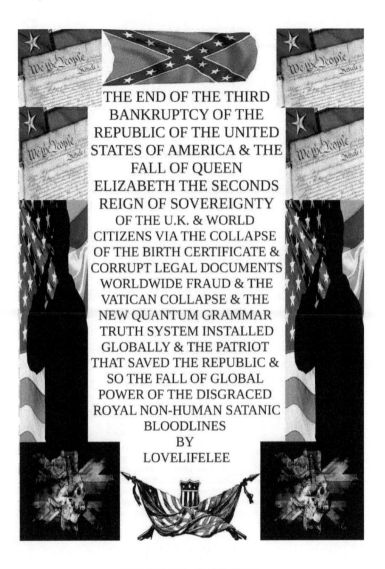

THE END OF THE THIRD
BANKRUPTCY OF THE
REPUBLIC OF THE UNITED
STATES OF AMERICA & THE
FALL OF QUEEN
ELIZABETH THE SECONDS
REIGN OF SOVEREIGNTY
OF THE U.K. & WORLD
CITIZENS VIA THE COLLAPSE
OF THE BIRTH CERTIFICATE &
CORRUPT LEGAL DOCUMENTS
WORLDWIDE FRAUD & THE
VATICAN COLLAPSE & THE
NEW QUANTUM GRAMMAR
TRUTH SYSTEM INSTALLED
GLOBALLY & THE PATRIOT
THAT SAVED THE REPUBLIC &
SO THE FALL OF GLOBAL
POWER OF THE DISGRACED
ROYAL NON-HUMAN SATANIC
BLOODLINES
BY
LOVELIFELEE

FRONT COVER

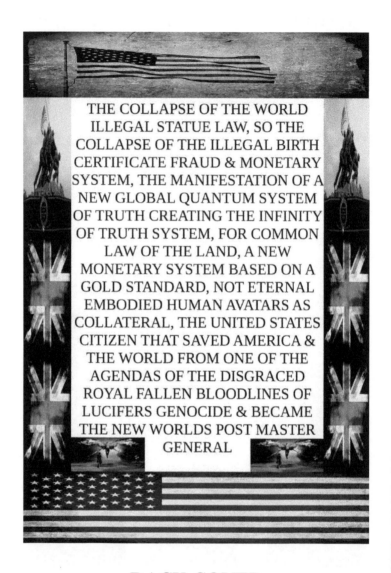

THE COLLAPSE OF THE WORLD
ILLEGAL STATUE LAW, SO THE
COLLAPSE OF THE ILLEGAL BIRTH
CERTIFICATE FRAUD & MONETARY
SYSTEM, THE MANIFESTATION OF A
NEW GLOBAL QUANTUM SYSTEM
OF TRUTH CREATING THE INFINITY
OF TRUTH SYSTEM, FOR COMMON
LAW OF THE LAND, A NEW
MONETARY SYSTEM BASED ON A
GOLD STANDARD, NOT ETERNAL
EMBODIED HUMAN AVATARS AS
COLLATERAL, THE UNITED STATES
CITIZEN THAT SAVED AMERICA &
THE WORLD FROM ONE OF THE
AGENDAS OF THE DISGRACED
ROYAL FALLEN BLOODLINES OF
LUCIFERS GENOCIDE & BECAME
THE NEW WORLDS POST MASTER
GENERAL

BACK COVER

THE TRUTH OF BIOLOGICAL CHEMICAL WEAPON INJECTIONS

& NASAL INOCULATIONS VIA TESTS & THE NEW NANO TECHNOLOGIES BEING INJECTED INTO HUMANITY TO PURPOSELY MAIM HARM KILL & REWRITE YOUR DNA ALTERING YOU TO TRANSHUMANISM WITHOUT YOUR CONSENT BY THE DISGRACED FALLEN ANGEL DESCENDANTS THEIR INTENTION TO HAVE A SMALL TRANSHUMANISM SLAVE

POPULATION & THEIR MASS GENOCIDE ON HUMANITY & THE INGREDIENTS & THE PERPETRATORS & AUTOIMMUNE RESPONSES & FUTURE NEURMBURG TRIALS & AN INTRODUCTION TO GROW YOUR ETERNAL LIGHT BODY

**BY
LOVELIFELEE**

FRONT COVER

Biological Chemical Injections known as vaccines the truth of this Eugenics Programs Agenda, the Ingredients put in Weapon Vaccines & the reactions the biological avatar body has when these CHEMICAL WARFARE WEAPONS are delivered by injections, the Autoimmune System Response & the New Biological Nano Technology Chemical Weapon Injections to Genocide Humanity, by Rewriting the RNA that builds the DNA with NO OFF SWITCH, this is to kill as many as possible on earth & CONTROL the survivors mind & body controlled via NANO TECHNOLOGIES injected into

your biological avatar bodies, This means after receiving the new non-vaccines bio-weapon you will no longer be of the original human DNA gene pool, and an introduction to the DNA blueprint of instructions to grow your eternal light body.

BACK COVER

OTHERS BOOKS BY LOVELIFELEE

THE BIOLOGY & CHEMISTRY & MEDICAL FRAUD EXPOSED

& THE TRUTH OF BACTERIA & VIRUSES & ALKALISED HEALING OF THE BIOLOGICAL AVATAR BODY, MEANING THE COLLAPSE OF THE PHARMACEUTICAL INDUSTRY, THE WHOLE MEDICAL BASIS OF TEACHING STANDARD WILL COLLAPSE AS WELL AS

UNIVERSITIES AND EDUCATION SYSTEMS, A NEW/ANCIENT NATURAL WAY TO HEAL, DIET IS KEY TO HAVE WELL BEING TO BE IN FULL HEALTH, TO EVOLVE ASCEND TRANSCEND TO BECOME ILLUMINATED TO ACCESS YOUR ETERNAL LIGHT BODY BY LOVELIFELEE

FRONT COVER

BACK COVER

The Biology and Chemistry Fraud
Exposed & The Truth of Bacteria and
Viruses and Alkalised Healing Of The
Biological Avatar Body, meaning the Fall
of the Pharmaceutical Industry, the whole
Medical Basis of Teaching Standard Will
Collapse as well as all Universities and
Education Systems. Also information of
the introduction to grow your eternal
light body via your schematic blueprint
instructions in your DNA and general
information on physical and mental well
being, practices, disciplines to run at your
biological and

chemical and electrical optimal levels to
access your eternal light body and then
able to access the hyper-dimensional
matrix of creation in its entirety, all
dimensions of The Brahman, The Whole,
The Creation and the eternal realms the
kingdom of light, that resides
Outside time and space
by
lovelifelee.

ACCESS YOUR
LIGHT BODY
VIA
THE MUNAY-KI
NINE RITES OF
INITIATION VIA
THE SOMATIC
BLUEPRINT IN YOUR DNA
&

ATION OF THE
COSMIC ENERGETIC
FIELD WE ARE CREATED
FROM AND BORN INTO

BY
LOVELIFELEE

FRONT COVER

THIS BOOK DISCUSSES AND GIVES AN
EXPLANATION OF THE COSMOS THE UNIVERSE,
OUR UNIVERSITY OF VIBRATING LIGHT, A
HOLOGRAM FOR SOULS TO COME AND EXPERIENCE
AND PAY KARMIC DEPTS OFF, IT GIVES AN
EXPLANATION OF THE COSMIC ENERGETIC FIELD
WE ARE CREATED FROM AND BORN INTO.
DISCUSSED ARE THE FOUR FUNDAMENTAL FORCES
OF CREATION THAT OF ELECTROMAGNETISM,
GRAVITY, THE STRONG AND WEAK NUCLEAR
FORCES, AND HOW THE SACRED GEOMETRIC
STRUCTURE OF FORM IS CREATED, THE SACRED
GEOMETRY STRUCTURE THE BUILDING BLOCKS OF
THE SCAFFOLDING OF LIFE.
DISCUSSED IS HOW WE EVOLVE AND ASCEND,
TRANSCEND AND METAMORPHOSIS INTO OUR
NATURAL STATE OF ETERNAL ANGELIC DIVINE LIGHT
BEINGS.HOW WE CAN TRANSCEND TIME AND SPACE
AND BE FULLY EMBODIED ON A 4th/5th DIMENSIONAL
PLANET EARTH BUT ACCESS OUR LUMINOUS LIGHT
BODIES AND TRAVEL IN ANY SPACE OR TIME WE
CHOOSE TO ACCESS AT WILL.
DISCUSSED IS HOW TO ACCESS YOUR LIGHT BODY
WITH THE MUNAY-KI NINE RITES OF INITIATION VIA
THE SCHEMATIC BLUEPRINT IN YOUR DNA, VIA
PRACTICES OF FIRE CEREMONY, MEDITATION, AND
WORKING WITH ENERGY AND LIGHT, WORKING WITH
THE FOUR FUNDAMENTAL PRINCIPLE FORCES OF
CREATION, AND ACCESSING LUMINOUS BEINGS
THAT WILL GUIDE YOU AND TEACH YOU AS YOU
COME TO A TIME OF TRANSFORMATION, A TIME OF
EVOLVING AND HEALING, TO ACCESS YOUR
ETERNAL LIGHT BODY, BLESSINGS NAMASTE
LOVELIFELEE.

BACK COVER

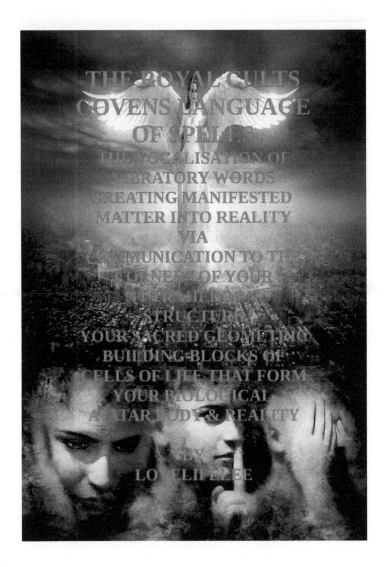

THE ROYAL CULTS
COVENS LANGUAGE
OF SPELLS
THE VOCALISATION OF
VIBRATORY WORDS
CREATING MANIFESTED
MATTER INTO REALITY
VIA
COMMUNICATION TO THE
CORNERS OF YOUR
ATOMIC IONIC
STRUCTURE
YOUR SACRED GEOMETRIC
BUILDING BLOCKS OF
CELLS OF LIFE THAT FORM
YOUR BIOLOGICAL
AVATAR BODY & REALITY
BY
LOVELIFELEE

FRONT COVER

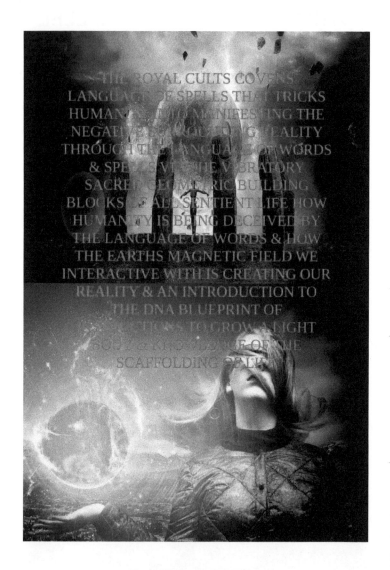

THE ROYAL CULTS COVERS
LANGUAGE OF SPELLS THAT TRICKS
HUMANITY INTO MANIFESTING THE
NEGATIVE EGO GROUND REALITY
THROUGH THE LANGUAGE OF WORDS
& SPELLS OF THE VIBRATORY
SACRED GEOMETRIC BUILDING
BLOCKS OF ALL SENTIENT LIFE HOW
HUMANITY IS BEING DECEIVED BY
THE LANGUAGE OF WORDS & HOW
THE EARTHS MAGNETIC FIELD WE
INTERACTIVE WITH IS CREATING OUR
REALITY & AN INTRODUCTION TO
THE DNA BLUEPRINT OF
INSTRUCTIONS TO GROW A LIGHT
BODY & KNOWLEDGE OF THE
SCAFFOLDING SPELL

BACK COVER

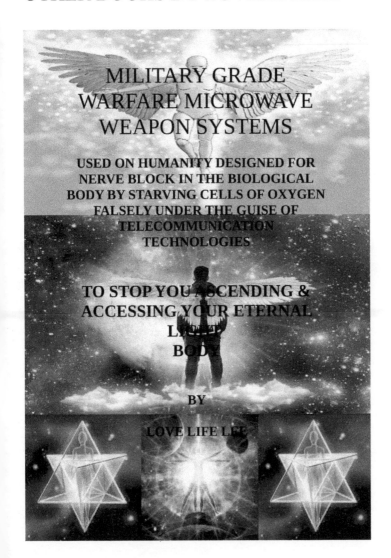

MILITARY GRADE
WARFARE MICROWAVE
WEAPON SYSTEMS

USED ON HUMANITY DESIGNED FOR
NERVE BLOCK IN THE BIOLOGICAL
BODY BY STARVING CELLS OF OXYGEN
FALSELY UNDER THE GUISE OF
TELECOMMUNICATION
TECHNOLOGIES

TO STOP YOU ASCENDING &
ACCESSING YOUR ETERNAL
LIGHT
BODY

BY

LOVE LIFE LEE

FRONT COVER

This short book exposes the military grade warfare microwave weapons systems in your homes 3G,4G and under the lying guise of telecommunications technologies 5G which are actually military microwave weapons designed to cause nerve block and starve the body of oxygen and can stop the heart, and manifesting our future reality.
Discussed also is understanding your cells their makeup and functions and their relationship to poisons especially microwave radiation poisoning.
An introduction to the DNA blueprint of instructions to grow a light body.

BACK COVER

OTHER BOOKS BY LOVELIFELEE

VEGAN RECIPES

PLANTS
ARE MEDICINE

PLANT FOOD FOR
YOUR CELLS THAT
FUEL & BUILD YOUR
SACRED GEOMETRIC
STRUCTURE

THE
SCAFFOLDING OF
LIFE

THATS
REGENERATING ON
A CONTINUUM

BY
LOVELIFELEE

FRONT COVER

THROUGH A VEGAN
DIET GAIN ACCESS TO
YOUR LIGHT BODY.
VEGAN FOOD FUELS
THE DODECAHEDRONS
WITH AMINO ACIDS &
THE TETRAHEDRONS
WITH PROTEINS, THESE
SACRED GEOMETRIC
STRUCTURES ARE THE
BUILDING BLOCKS OF,
THE SCAFFOLDING OF
LIFE YOUR BIOLOGICAL
HUMAN AVATAR, THESE
FOODS & VEGAN
RECIPES WILL FUEL
YOUR BODY & WITH
OTHER SPIRITUAL
PRACTICES &
MEDITATION YOU WILL
ACCESS YOUR
ETERNAL LIGHT BODY.

DIET IS KEY

BY
LOVELIFELEE

BACK COVER

234

OTHER BOOKS BY LOVELIFELEE

FRONT COVER

LEARN ABOUT
PLANT MEDICINES &
MAKE YOUR OWN
BE YOUR OWN
DOCTOR FOR YOU
ARE AN ETERNAL
LIGHT BEING

HEAL THE CELLS OF
YOUR BIOLOGICAL
HUMAN AVATAR
BODY WITH
NATURAL PLANT
MEDICINES

PLANT MEDICINE &
DIET IS KEY TO
ACCESSING YOUR
LUMINOUS ENERGY
FIELD & RAISING
YOUR OVERALL
VIBRATION THEN
RAISING YOUR
CONSCIOUSNESS AND
OPENING YOUR
LIGHT BODY

LOVE LIFE LEE

BACK COVER

236

OTHER BOOKS BY LOVELIFELEE

POEMS OF MAGICAL WONDER

POEMS MAGICAL IN NATURE

POEMS OF SPLENDOUR

FROM THE MINDS EYE & HEART SPACE

OF LOVE LIFE LEE

SOME OF MY MAGICAL LIFE JOURNEY

EXPERIENCES OF SHAMANIC CEREM

AYAHUASCA CEREMONY'S

PLANT MEDICINE , DREAMS , MEDITATIONS

REMOTE VIEWING , OUT OF BODY JOURNEY'S

AND LIFE EXPERIENCE'S

POEMS AND TRUTHS
OF OUR HOLOGRAPHIC UNIVERSE

THE PHOTON THE LIGHT PARTICLE
IN WHICH WE EXIST AND RESIDE UNTILL
WE EXPAND WITH LIGHT BRIGHTENING
SHINING BRIGHT IN OUR BODYS OF LIGHT

ILLUMINATED OUR RAINBOW BODY's FREE
ANGELS WE BE IMMORTAL
INTERDIMENSIONAL
LIGHT BEINGS OF CONSCIOUS ENERGY

BY LOVE LIFE LEE

LOVE LIFE LEE
YO RASTA !
LOVE LIFE LEE
LIFE LIFE TO THE FULL
FOR ETERNITY
CHANTING AND DANCING
IS WHAT YOU DO BEST
MEDITATION WITH THE SPIRIT'S
YOU TRULY BLESSED
HEAD FULL OF KNOWLEDGE
HEART OF GOLD
WHEN THE GODS MADE YOU
THEY HAD TO BREAK THE MOULD
COS LETS FACE IT DUDE
AND WE ALL AGREE
THIS WORLD CAN ONLY HANDLE
ONE LOVE LIFE LEE

FRONT COVER

237

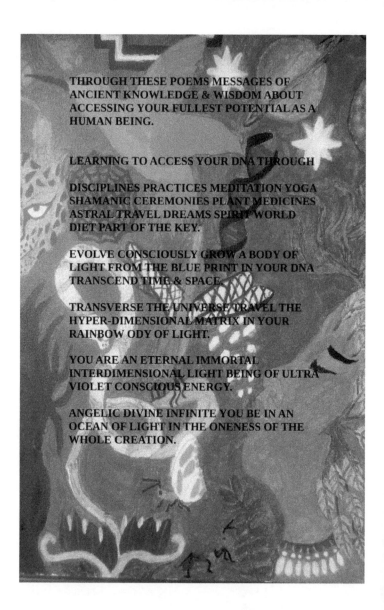

THROUGH THESE POEMS MESSAGES OF
ANCIENT KNOWLEDGE & WISDOM ABOUT
ACCESSING YOUR FULLEST POTENTIAL AS A
HUMAN BEING.

LEARNING TO ACCESS YOUR DNA THROUGH

DISCIPLINES PRACTICES MEDITATION YOGA
SHAMANIC CEREMONIES PLANT MEDICINES
ASTRAL TRAVEL DREAMS SPIRIT WORLD
DIET PART OF THE KEY.

EVOLVE CONSCIOUSLY GROW A BODY OF
LIGHT FROM THE BLUE PRINT IN YOUR DNA
TRANSCEND TIME & SPACE.

TRANSVERSE THE UNIVERSE TRAVEL THE
HYPER-DIMENSIONAL MATRIX IN YOUR
RAINBOW ODY OF LIGHT.

YOU ARE AN ETERNAL IMMORTAL
INTERDIMENSIONAL LIGHT BEING OF ULTRA
VIOLET CONSCIOUS ENERGY.

ANGELIC DIVINE INFINITE YOU BE IN AN
OCEAN OF LIGHT IN THE ONENESS OF THE
WHOLE CREATION.

BACK COVER

238

OTHER BOOKS BY LOVELIFELEE

FRONT COVER

Expressions of life's journey, poems of
mystical experiences on my life's path
on planet Gaia & beyond.
Experiences of travelling around the world
and off world in the hyper-dimensional
matrix, some from in this universe & other
eternal realms. Experiences from
meditations, ancient spiritual practices,
plant medicines of Ayahuasca, Magic
Mushrooms, Salvia Divinorum, and
different forms of DMT
Dimethyltryptamine leaving my body
instantly travelling down wormholes
entering different dimensions of reality of
this holographical light university &
realities of the true nature outside time &
space in the eternal realm, poems of your
immortal light body & the hyper-
dimensional matrix the whole of the
brahman the creation Namaste lovelifelee

MER -KA -BA

BACK COVER

FRONT COVER

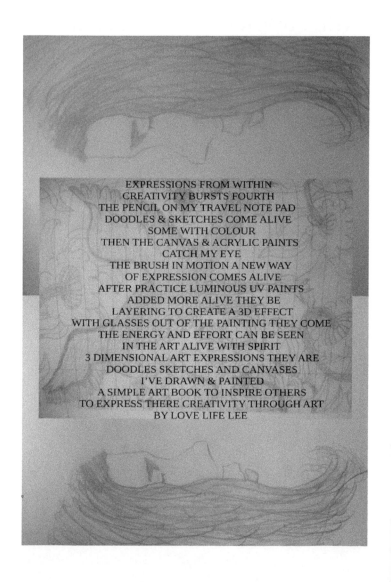

EXPRESSIONS FROM WITHIN
CREATIVITY BURSTS FOURTH
THE PENCIL ON MY TRAVEL NOTE PAD
DOODLES & SKETCHES COME ALIVE
SOME WITH COLOUR
THEN THE CANVAS & ACRYLIC PAINTS
CATCH MY EYE
THE BRUSH IN MOTION A NEW WAY
OF EXPRESSION COMES ALIVE
AFTER PRACTICE LUMINOUS UV PAINTS
ADDED MORE ALIVE THEY BE
LAYERING TO CREATE A 3D EFFECT
WITH GLASSES OUT OF THE PAINTING THEY COME
THE ENERGY AND EFFORT CAN BE SEEN
IN THE ART ALIVE WITH SPIRIT
3 DIMENSIONAL ART EXPRESSIONS THEY ARE
DOODLES SKETCHES AND CANVASES
I'VE DRAWN & PAINTED
A SIMPLE ART BOOK TO INSPIRE OTHERS
TO EXPRESS THERE CREATIVITY THROUGH ART
BY LOVE LIFE LEE

BACK COVER

OTHER BOOK COMING 2021
FIVE YEAR PROCESS

FRONT COVER

THE MOTHER SPIRIT OF AYAHUASCA
MEDICINE A POWER PLANT HEALER &
TEACHER SHE BE CLEANSING THE BODY MIND
& SPIRIT SHE BE CONNECTING YOU TO
NATURE TO SPIRIT THE ETERNAL MAGICAL
SHE BE INSIDE ARE SOME OF MY TALES OF
MY JOURNEY TO THE AMAZON RAINFOREST
IN PERU & AYAHUASCA CEREMONIES AND
EXPERIENCES

BACK COVER

BOOK PAGE INDEX

DISCLAIMER

I am a critical thinker and a critical researcher of all matters of truths of existence, I am spirit the essence of the expression of the divine creator of the oneness of existence, I am an essense of gravity, I am love, I am light, I eternally create matter on a continuum from the four fundamental energies of electromagnetism gravity the weak & strong nuclear forces, creating physical form with the structures of dodecahedrons & tetrahedrons to create the building blocks of the scaffolding of life, therefore I am not the body or the mind, its is a living holographical avatar, I exist outside time and space in the eternal realm in the kingdom of light, I am multidimensional and fractal in essence, manifesting metamorphosing shapeshifting into a three dimensional human avatar form in the now, the present moment inside time & space in this holographical university of vibrating light, a reality of energetic resonance, we are one in the oneness of the whole, the brahman, the creation, in service to the oneness, blessings on your awakening of consciousness & on your journey of enlightenment from the path of mortality to immortality for the truth be, we are eternal immortal interdimensional light beings of ultra violet divine energetic consciousness, so consciously evolve by tapping into our DNA schematic blueprint instructions to grow our eternal light bodies, then ascending, transcending, metamorphosis then ensues to your eternal rainbow light being natural state of being, returning home once again a caretaker, a guardian of all galaxies races and species in the cosmos, a star keeper & a guardian creator of the creation the braham the whole, namaste blessings lovelifelee

PS. With Supreme power of the divine essence I claim my own sovereignty over my human avatar body mind soul, my eternal spirit, I claim Supreme power with the energy of the divine spirit of ultra violet conscious energy that I am a sovereignty of the divine, I rule my own affairs in the parameters of universal law, karmic law, law of attraction, divine and sacred law, & universal Natural law which is law of the land, law of natural living breathing man/woman, so an eternal light being residing in a human biological avatar, namaste love & light lovelifelee.

I being sovereignty of my entire spirit eternal light being human body, am not bound by illegal criminal corporation corporate law which is statute law, law of contracts, these laws taken from admiralty law also known as maritime law more commonly known as law of the sea, I am not lost at sea, dead or in limbo, I AM LIVING, LIVE, ANIMATED in EXISTENCE, therefore I do not enter into verbal or written or any contract, to any corporation, I do not sign say or agree with any contracts from these devious bodies or entities, as my earth born biological parents were tricked with out there knowledge and deceived without their consent, to get a birth certificate of slavery, which is not the eternal spirit me connected to the birth certificate is an illusionary character which can only be created by introducing MR MASTER MISS MRS and in conjunction using CAPITAL LETTERS on your BIRTH NAME and FAMILY name, so example MR JOE BLOGGS, so therefore I do not agree to the false title of Mr that's followed by my alleged legal name on the birth certificate, so therefore I am not agreeing to be a legal person which is a corporation, which is an artificial person, not living, being in physical reality, an illusion, non-existant, so I do not agree I am not an artificial person, and I am not agreeing to be under statue law which is an artificial person not in existence, not alive, so fictional which in turn puts you under illegal statute law. I AM GOVERNED BY

UNIVERSAL LAW, KARMIC LAW, NATURAL LAW, LAW OF ATTRACTION, SACRED LAW & UNIVERSAL COMMON LAW WHICH IS LAW OF THE LAND which we are governed by on earth by OUR OWN SUPREME DIVINE POWER, OVER SOVEREIGNTY of MIND BODY SOUL, so that of our ETERNAL SPIRIT ESSENCE that of our IMMORTAL DIVINE ULTRA VIOLET ENERGETIC CHI ETERNAL CONSCIOUSNESS that resides in this BIOLOGICAL HUMAN AVATAR BODY in the NOW the PRESENT MOMENT.

A LEGAL NAME I AM NOT A LEGAL PERSON I AM NOT I AM NOT OWNED BY A CORPORATION I AM A LIVING MAN, but I TRULY am a Divine Sentient being, I am an not the body or mind, I am an ETERNAL IMMORTAL BEING OF LIGHT energised by my ULTRA VIOLET DIVINE ENERGETIC CONSCIOUSNESS, I am god conscious,

I declare sovereignty by my supreme god consciousness power and authority of my self and my being in its entirety, in my eternal spirit essence in my complete wholeness in my entirety of all my multidimensional facets of my being, and as my DNA flashes a 100 Herz a second, as my DNA flashes light a hundred times every second, I am a divine angelic light being connected to the oneness of all creation in its entirety, inside time and space and outside time and space, from the eternal immortal realms, I do not recognise this illegal corrupt court system of the law of the sea transformed to the law of the land, that is a corporate entity and was set up by the invading extraterrestrial two Royal Fallen Angel Goldsmith Davidic Zionest Israelite Satanic Demonic bloodlines, of the House of Saud and the British German Nazi European familes, that are also known as the two controlling mafia families Ashkenazi and Kahazarian crime families.

NAMASTE AMEN BLESSINGS TO ALL SENTIENT LIFE IN THE ONENESS OF CREATION THE BRAHMAN THE WHOLE, may none suffer from sorrow and be liberated as the ripe bearing fruit on a vine is so, and may you leave darkness being lead to light, amd transition from mortality to immortality may you be illuminated and blessed eternally Namaste LoveLifeLee.

ONCE YOU"VE ACCESSED GOD CONSCIOUSNESS THEY THE NEGATIVE ENTITIES FORCES ARE DISPELLED FROM YOUR EXISTENCE & THEY CEASE TO BE IN EXISTENCE

Once you have accessed god consciousness and accessed different dimensions of reality astral travelling, remote viewing, communed with other entities, leaving the body in various state like meditation, divine sacred medicinal plants, accessing the hyperdimensional matrix inside time and space and also outside time and space, in the eternal realms, and like my self many light workers and earth keepers are creating micro universes and opening portholes outside of this universe and outside time and space to the eternal realms, to allow light beings buddha beings, some are humans that have stopped the karmic cycles of life and death and accessed their light body and ascended, transcended, the portholes allows a bridge for them to access this dimension into this low 3rd dimension reality, they will guide, heal, and teach you they are there to help in your transformation, to assist you, as you metamorphosis back to your true divine natural state of being as an and eternal fully embodied human light being, the divine essense of the expression of the creator of the eternal oneness of creation, as many of us have and are doing so in the present, there is nothing the evil dark negative forces can do, for you are reconnected to nature, spirit, the eternal essense of the divine creator. And therefore GOD CONSCIOUS Namaste LoveLifeLee.

THOUSANDS & THOUSANDS OF SUBJECTS THAT I'VE STUDIED to come to a individual conclusion of the god conscious mind realization of true facts, with logic, common sense, this book was born, with the intent to educate truth of history and other books I've written to stop our humanities light being family toxicing there avatar biological bodies & minds, so creating health, harmony, equilibrium, in the body, inturn the mind & spirit this then manifests into the whole of humanities co-consciousness, and manifested reality changes to a peaceful, more content way of being & expressing from within into the electromagnetic field of creation, Namaste.

END

These statements and forms at back of book are for you to cut out of book and use in daily life, if you feel the need to do so, for your Unalienable Sovereignty Rights and for the security and for your own protection and that of your local community and its citizens.

Namaste I wish Consciousness and manifest Blessing to all of Humanities Eternal Light Being Citizens and all Sentient Life in the Creation lovelifelee.

I also recommend you to registar your birth certificate at Common Law Court & any businesses you own, and take ownership of your fictitious strawman created by the government.

1

ARE YOU UNDER OATH OFFICER
YES OR NO, then say NO I do not
understand you , I do (not-stand) under
you, I am a Sentient Spiritual Being of
Light I am in the present manifested in
this human biological avatar body, for
this life times experience, I am a natural
living breathing man/woman living under
the Eternal Common Law, Law of the
Land which is Natural Law I am also
bound by Universal Law, Karmic Law
and bound by Law of Attraction. And
officer you Swore an Oath to the
Constitution which is Common Law and
are bound by your Sworn Oath, So
therefore gentlemen you are not dealing
with a fictitious corporate entity I do not
consent contract with you, for I have
accessed God Consciousness, therefore
good day may you be blessed eternally,
namaste.

2

You can tell the statute officers that in the English language, Do You Understand, means do you comprehend what I am saying to you?. But in the trickery language of Legalese it has been changed to actually mean, Do you stand under me?, actually meaning, DO YOU GRANT ME AUTHORITY OVER YOU SO THAT YOU HAVE TO OBEY WHATEVER I TELL YOU TO DO!

And your reponse is NO I DO NOT CONSENT, I DO NOT UNDERSTAND YOU, I DO NOT CONSENT TO CONTRACT.

3

You can also tell them and say to the Statute Law officers this statement –

In CONSTITUTIONAL LAW – The Government is brought into existence by THE PEOPLE – But it is known that the main three tiers of government cannot bring in or create any ACTS, STATUES, GUIDELINES, or any REGULATIONS – That can INFRINGE on NATURAL LAW rights, so cannot be encroached upon in a way that violates NATURAL LAW – This means corporate statue officers enforcing criminal and illegitimate unlawful corporate Statute Law cannot Impringe their will on you as to impinge is to come into contact or encroach or have an impact and to infringe is to encroach on a right or privilege or to violate THE NATURAL LAW RIGHTS we receive from BIRTH. Infringe as a verb abuse of a privilege, abuse of one's rights, advance stealthily (meaning deception of words to get you into and illegitimate unlawful corporate Statute Law contract by trickery of words deceit there game), aggress, arrogate, breach, break bounds, break upon, break into, commit a CRIME against our BIRTH given NATURAL LAW rights, our INALIENABLE RIGHTS.

So NATURAL LAW rights which are INALIENABLE rights, which are (PERSONAL RIGHTS that cannot be ignored), given to us citizens of humanity on this planet Gaia our Mother Earth, Pachamama, these rights are given to us at birth and can never be taken away and those freedoms and rights include – FREE SPEECH – FREEDOM TO THINK – FREEDOM OF ASSOCIATION – FREEDOM OF ASSEMBLY – BODY INTEGRITY and access to JUSTICE – These rights CAN NEVER BE TAKEN AWAY.

So you the individual start using these rights and INVOKE them when interacting with criminal illegitimate corporate Statute Law enforcing officers, by always starting with – ARE YOU UNDER OATH OFFICER, ARE YOU ACTING UNDER YOUR OATH of CONSTITUTIONAL LAW, YOUR OATH OF COMMON LAW, YOU'RE YOUR OATH OF NATURAL LAW – Which is UNIVERSAL LAW, yes or no officer.

4

WHAT TO SAY TO THE ILLEGITIMATE UNLAWFUL CRIMINAL CORPORATION ENFORCER POLICE OFFICER & OTHER ENFORCING AGENTS

When interacting with the criminal corporation enforcing officers – You would say to them – ARE YOU ACTING UNDER OATH OFFICER – If they do not answer which many do not and try to avoid answering, YOU SAY – YES or NO are you acting under OATH officer, then some times there Ego gets bruised and then if an officer trys to arrest you and detain you, YOU SHOULD SAY – I'M GOING TO VIDEO YOU – They will say you can not video me, they will even say in certain locations, you can't film me in this train station or airport or outside a police station, and then YOU SAY – YES I CAN VIDEO YOU because if you are COMMITING A CRIME as a SERVANT or CIVIL SERVANT or an OATH TAKER, that get there salary from the government, that we The People the citizens are paying, THEN I CAN FILM, VIDEO and RECORD for preservation for legal DOCUMENT MANUSCRIPT EVIDENCE RECORDS.

Then if the officer insists you cant video film them that they have all these guidelines, YOU SAY – NO NO NO GUIDELINES can not INFRINGE PERSONAL RIGHTS, UNDER CONSTITUTIONAL LAW which you swore an OATH to, which is NATURAL LAW and so by Universal Law.

IF A CRIMINAL CORPORATION ENFORCING OFFICER TRYS TO ARREST & HANDCUFF YOU – THIS IS WHAT TO SAY

When an officer starts to enter your personal space SAY TO THEM – I DO NOT CONSENT, if you touch me with hand cuffs as I've informed you I DO NOT CONSENT, I DO NOT CONSENT TO BEING STOPPED – Then usually an officer will go in front of you or try and block you from movement of physical travel, then YOU SAY – I DO NOT CONSENT TO YOU STOPPING ME and I DO NOT CONSENT TO YOU PHYSICALLY TOUCHING ME, MY BODY, MY PERSON – then YOU SHOULD SAY – If You Put CUFFS On Me That is a CRIME of BATTERY, because I have Rights If YOU PHYSICALLY TOUCH ME or STOP my MOVEMENT, STOP me

TRAVELLING, you OFFICER are ACTING OUTSIDE your OATH, that is UNLAWFUL as you know as you took the CONSTITUTIONAL LAW OATH, the OATH of NATURAL LAW, which is UNIVERSAL LAW.

Continue SAYING – ACTING outside of your OATH this is UNLAWFUL – If you touch me or put hand cuffs on me that is a CRIME of BATTERY which is Five years in prison.
If a Police Officer does something UNLAWFUL – They are actually going outside of their PROTECTION of the POLICE.
If an Officer does not answer that they are under OATH when asked or try to avoid the answer to that question, it then logical to assume that the officer knows that what they are doing is UNLAWFUL, and if an officer admits to doing UNLAWFUL behaviour and therefore COMMITING a CRIME, then they can go to prison for up to TWENTY years, for being in Police Uniform

COMMITING a CRIME.

When an officer does not answer that they are under OATH and when they are about to put hand cuffs on, you Film, Video Record them, then SAY –
OFFICER YOU ARE NOW ENTERING INTO CONTRACT and MY said hourly RATE IS 5000.00 Pounds an Hour (you can choose any amount as they are ENTERING into CONTRACT and YOU DO NOT CONSENT).
Then YOU SAY to the Officer – It will cost you 5000.00 Pounds an Hour and there are (if this is the case more than one officer present) four officers present, so this RATE will apply personally individually to each officer present, so the hourly cost will be 20,000.00 Per Hour, if you illegally and criminally detain me without my CONSENT.

If the officer (s) do Commit the Crime of BATTERY and by doing so also commit the crime of KIDNAP by illegally and criminally hand cuffing you without your

Consent and detain you after say three hours of illegal and criminal detainment, YOU SHOULD SAY to the officer (s) – That all officers will be CHARGED the said RATE of the Initial contact, when I did not CONSENT and told them that they were ENTERING CONTRACT with YOU against your then STATED NON-CONSENT, and that they are now going to be charged individually up to this said time (for three hours of illegitimate unlawful detainment) 15,000.00 Pounds each, so collectively four officers equals 60,000.00 Pound Invoice in total.

As you were told The Said Hourly Rate Cost when you ENTERED into CONTRACT against my CONSENT at the initial contact three hours prior to my illegitimate unlawful and criminal detention, when you ILLEGALLY broke your OATH, so COMMITING a CRIME, One of the Crimes being of Battery, another being the Crime of Kiddnapping.

So next YOU MUST SAY – I ALSO INFORM YOU THAT I WILL NOT BE

PAYING ANY FINES as they are UNLAWFUL, and CRIMINAL in nature under NATURAL LAW, (then state the time frame of prison sentence for that Crime and maximum Fine) – I believe its six months in prison and up to a 10,000.00 Fine for that Crime.

Then YOU SHOULD SAY – I WILL BE CHARGING every hour to each individual officer, including preparing the case, with the Said 5000.00 Pounds Hourly Rate. If it takes 10 hour days for five days that charge would be 250,000.00 plus damages costs and payment of your legal fees plus the charges of the initial arrest, it expensive, to illegitimately unlawfully criminally commit a crime on a citizen and while in a police officers uniform that is long prison sentences as well as huge financial loss even bankruptcy. If the citizen knows and understands the Common Law and Statute Law you can stand in your Sovereignty Power, and take the case to Common Law Court of Justice and you will win, win in High Court and Supreme

Court. The police fear the loss of there personal wealth and imprisonment and so will heed or should heed or it could destoy there lives, on many levels.
Next you need to tell the officers the next procedure after that will be that the case will go to High Court and the Supreme Court and that you will WIN the case, because each officer Acted Unlawful there by Commiting the Crimes of – UNLAWFUL DETENTION, KIDNAPPING, the Crime of BATTERY.

Then YOU SHOULD SAY – And any police officer Acting Under OATH knows that being Additionally dressed up as a police officer, and Acting as an Officer but is Criminally Illegitimately Unlawfully Arresting Citizens is a CRIME so Punishable by up to TWENTY years in Prison.

6

THE OATH OF COMMON LAW COURT OFFICE

I (Individuals Name) swear I will truthfully and faithfully perform my obligated duties as an officer of this Common Law Court according to the principles of Natural Justice and the principles of Due Proccess, behaving and acting at all times with lawfulness, honesty and integrity.
I also recognize that if I fail to do so, to consistently abide by this said Oath I can and will be removed from my Office, of the Common Law Court.
I make this statement of the public Oath freely with clarity and without mental reservation with no uncertainty or ulterior motive or coercion.

7

The declaration model form is below –

I, _____, being of sound mind and of clear conscience, do hereby swear that I will absolutely truthfully and faithfully and justly perform and execute the office of an agent of the Common Law Court of Justice according to the absolute best of my abilities.

I understand that if I fail in my sworn duties or I am compromised or betray the trust and responsibilities of my office of the Common Law Court I will automatically forfeit my right to this position and can be dismissed immediately.

I take this serious and dignified solemn OATH freely with no reservations, with no ulterior motive and without coercion, according to my conscience as a free man or woman, and as a citizen under the authority and jurisdiction of the Common Law.

_____ Signature, SIGNED

_____ Date

_____ Common Law Court
Offical Stamp.

8

THE NOTICE & WARRANT TO
DEPUTIZE that is issued UNDER the
AUTHORITY of the SHERIFF-Officers
Office of the COMMON LAW COURT
of JUSTICE and under the
JURISDICTION of NATURAL LAW &
the LAW of NATIONS.

To all Peace Officers & all Officials of
Law & Enforcement Officers of Statute
Law –

This Public Notice is issued to you as a
lawful warrant by the Common Law
Court of Justice, placing you under the
jurisdiction of the Common Law Court
and Natural Justice, and deputizing you
as its Official Peace Officers.

Upon your taking of the official appended
sworn OATH of Common Law Court
Office, you are empowered to act as the
lawful agents and protectors of the

Common Law Court and all its proceedings, and are sworn to serve and enforce its, Warrants, Writs, Summons and Courts Orders on any and all Persons and Institutions, Corporations, companies named by the Common Law Court.

If you choose not to take this OATH of office to the Common Law Court Office, you are compelled and Ordered by the Common Law Court and by Natural Law to refrain from interfering with the actions of the Sheriff-Officer or other Peace Officers that are deputized and are legitimately & fully empowered to act for the Common Law Court of Justice.

If you resist, impede or disrupt the actions of the Common Law Court Orders or its Sworn Sheriff-officers or Peace Officers you can and will be CHARGED with CRIMINAL ASSAULT and OBSTRUCTION of JUSTICE.

Issued on_____ in the community of _____ by the following Legal Agent

or Sworn Peace Officer or Sheriff-officer
of the Common Law Court of Justice –
_____ Signature, SIGNED
_____ Common Law Courts
Offical Stamp.

9

PUBLIC NOTICE of CLAIM of RIGHT to be Publicly issued in order to convene and assemble a local Common Law Court.

Issued by _____ on the date of _____ in the community of _____.

I _____ give Public Notice of my personal claim of right and of my lawful excuse to convene and assemble and establish a Common Law Court under my liberty as an Eternal Spirit Light Being embodied as a Human Being, a flesh and blood man or woman, and hereby call upon the support of all competent men and women to assist me in this Lawful Right.

I further give Public Notice of my absolute personal Right of Claim and of my lawful excuse to convene and assemble and establish as part of such a court a jury of my peers, consisting of twelve men or women, to judge a matter of affairs affecting the well being, safety, rights, protection and security of myself and my community, that matter of affairs being of the following – The description of the said issue, also a statement of claim and the named parties.

I further give Public Notice that the said Jury of my peers claims the jurisdictional competence, capability and capacity to judge this matter of affairs and issue a verdict and a sentence within the said Common Law Court assembled and established to render such a judgement, based upon absolute proven and irrefutable evidence presented within its Common Law Court.

I hereby publicly advocate and so call upon and appeal and request the support of my community to assemble and establish this Common Law Court and its Jury of twelve men or women, to be sworn to act in such a capacity for the scope and duration of the Common Law Court proceedings, according to Natural Law and the rules of due process and evidence.

I make this Public Claim of Right freely without ulterior motive or coercion, in the public interest of Justice and in the interest of the Publics and the Communities Welfare.

_____ Claimant Signature
_____ Witness   Signature
_____ Date.

Lightning Source UK Ltd.
Milton Keynes UK
UKHW040939030822
406784UK00001B/227